T0108998

A New Look at Gender and Minority Differences in Officer Career Progression in the Military

Beth J. Asch, Trey Miller, Alessandro Malchiodi

Prepared for the Office of the Secretary of Defense

Approved for public release; distribution unlimited

NATIONAL DEFENSE RESEARCH INSTITUTE

The research described in this report was prepared for the Office of the Secretary of Defense (OSD). The research was conducted within the RAND National Defense Research Institute, a federally funded research and development center sponsored by OSD, the Joint Staff, the Unified Combatant Commands, the Navy, the Marine Corps, the defense agencies, and the defense Intelligence Community under Contract W74V8H-06-C-0002.

Library of Congress Cataloging-in-Publication Data is available for this publication.

ISBN: 978-0-8330-5937-6

Published 2012 by the RAND Corporation
1776 Main Street, P.O. Box 2138, Santa Monica, CA 90407-2138
1200 South Hayes Street, Arlington, VA 22202-5050
4570 Fifth Avenue, Suite 600, Pittsburgh, PA 15213-2665
RAND URL: http://www.rand.org/
To order RAND documents or to obtain additional information, contact
Distribution Services: Telephone: (310) 451-7002;
Fax: (310) 451-6915; Email: order@rand.org

Preface

In 2011, the congressionally mandated Military Leadership Diversity Commission concluded that two factors contributed to the underrepresentation among senior military leaders of racial/ethnic minority and female officers: lower rates of promotion than white male officers and, in the case of mid-level female officers, lower retention. Left unclear is the relative contribution of each factor. That is, to what extent is the lack of representation due mostly to lower retention, mostly to lower promotion rates, or to both? Furthermore, other factors might account for differences in promotion and retention outcomes, such as differences in source of commission, entry date, and occupational area. In the late 1990s, RAND analyzed the retention and promotion pipeline of minority and female officers and decomposed the pipeline into promotion versus retention outcomes, controlling for other factors. The study was conducted in support of the Department of Defense 1999 report on the Career Progression of Minority and Women Officers and used data on officer cohorts entering between 1967 and 1991, tracking them through 1994.

Because the results of this earlier study are dated, the Office of the Secretary of Defense asked RAND to update it, using more recent data. The updated analysis is summarized in this report. In addition, this study also estimated differences in the career progression of female officers in occupations partially closed to women relative to women's career progression in open occupations. It should be recognized that the study describes empirical differences in officer promotion and retention outcomes, but does not examine why these differences occur. These differences may occur because of differences in qualifications and/or opportunities, but the study does not provide evidence related to either of these factors. Therefore, it should be considered only as a first step toward a better understanding of career progression differences among officers. The analysis should be of interest to the policy community concerned about the career progression of minority and female officers and the military manpower research community.

The research was sponsored by the Director of Accession Policy within the Office of the Under Secretary of Defense for Personnel and Readiness and conducted within the Forces and Resources Policy Center of the RAND National Defense Research Institute, a federally funded research and development center sponsored by the Office of the Secretary of Defense, the Joint Staff, the Unified Combatant Commands, the Navy, the Marine Corps, the defense agencies, and the defense Intelligence Community.

For more information on the RAND Forces and Resources Policy Center, see http://www.rand.org/nsrd/ndri/centers/frp.html or contact the director (contact information is provided on the web page).

Contents

Tables

Summary

Although military accessions of women, blacks, Asians, Hispanics, and persons of other racial backgrounds have increased over time, the proportions of these groups in the senior officer corps remain relatively low. In fiscal year (FY) 2009, for example, these groups had a lower proportion of O1 to O3 officers than they had of accessions, a lower proportion of O4 to O6 officers than they had of O1 to O3 officers, and a lower proportion of general and flag officers than they had of O4 to O6 officers (Table S.1).

The Military Leadership Diversity Commission has concluded that two contributors to the underrepresentation of women and racial and ethnic minorities among senior military leaders are their lower rates of promotion and retention relative to those for white males. This research explores the relative contribution of each of these factors.

RAND research conducted in the late 1990s found that women had lower promotion and retention rates than white men and that black men, in comparison with white men, had lower promotion but similar retention rates. Focus groups conducted for the earlier work found that women perceived themselves to have limited occupational roles and had concerns about harassment and family obligations. Black officers reported difficulty in forming peer and mentor relationships and were more likely to receive assignments, such as recruiting, that were not typical for their occupation.

Since then, several policies and events have affected military careers, including retention and promotion opportunities. The drawdown of the 1990s reduced retention and promotion opportunities. The September 2001 terrorist attacks against the United States and the subsequent military operations in Iraq and Afghanistan changed perceptions about military service

Table S.1
Active Component Officer Corps, by Gender, Race, and Ethnicity Status, FY 2009 (%)

Service	Accessions	O1 to O3	O4 to O6	General and Flag Officers	All Officers
Female	20.58	17.96	12.72	5.60	16.21
White	75.81	77.27	83.71	92.97	78.86
Black	9.19	8.90	8.13	5.82	8.74
Asian	4.93	4.01	2.53	0.44	3.74
Other, two or more, unknown	10.07	9.81	5.73	0.77	8.66
Hispanic	5.59	5.59	4.11	1.32	5.20

SOURCE: Department of Defense, 2011, Tables B-23, B-27, B-38, and B-39.

and had a negative effect on high-quality enlistments. (No similar information is available about officer accessions.) At the same time, military pay and benefits, which lagged those in the private sector in the 1990s, have increased relative to civilian pay in the past decade. The services have also undertaken several efforts to improve officer diversity.

Given these and other changes, the Under Secretary of Defense for Personnel and Readiness asked RAND to update its earlier research, with attention as well to the career progression of women in military occupations that are partially closed. By *partially closed*, we mean occupations that are deemed open to women but that have some positions for which assignment of women is restricted. This report summarizes our findings. Below we describe our data and methods, our results, and our conclusions.

Data and Methods

We use the Proxy-PERSTEMPO data file maintained by the Defense Manpower Data Center. The data include information on officer service, occupation, grade, months to current grade, source of commission, deployments, dates of entry and of commission, and such demographic variables as race, ethnicity, gender, marital status, and education.

We estimate differences in retention and promotion between white males (the reference group) and several other groups defined by race, Hispanic origin, and sex. The race groups were defined as white, black, and other minority; because of small sample sizes, we group Asians, Pacific Islanders, and others into the other minority category. We also examine how women have progressed as officers in ground-combat occupations that are closed to them at lower levels. We controlled for several variables—including service, source of commission, prior enlisted status, occupation group, deployment experience, marital status, and education—in our analyses to separate the effects of race, ethnicity, gender, and, for restricted occupations, occupation on career progression.

It is important to recognize that the analysis provides descriptions of how career progression differs by race, ethnicity, and gender and by whether an occupation is partially closed to women. The analysis does not attempt to explain why these differences occur. It also does not attempt to ascertain whether minority or female officers with identical characteristics as white male officers (our reference group) have different career progressions. This is because we do not control for every relevant factor that could affect differences in career progression between white males and the other groups we consider. These other factors include, for example, entry characteristics, such as aptitude, and performance and assignment opportunities once in service. Similarly, the analysis also does not attempt to ascertain whether opening occupations to women affects their career progression. Because the analyses are purely descriptive, readers should not interpret any of the findings as causal.

Minority and Gender Differences in Career Progression

Among male officers, blacks, Hispanics, and other minorities are generally less likely than white males to be promoted (Table S.2). These differences appear to be somewhat greater at higher levels, e.g., from O4 to O5. Nevertheless, retention rates for minority male officers, given promotion to a specified level, are somewhat greater than for white males, especially at

Table S.2
Estimated Percentage Point Differences in the Likelihood of Reaching Promotion and Retention Milestones for Male Officers

Milestone	Percentage of White Male Officers Retained/ Promoted	Percentage Point Difference: Minority Male Officers – White Male Officers		
		Black Males	Hispanic Males	Other Minority Males
Promotion				
O1 to O2	98.5	−1.1***	−0.5***	−0.1
O2 to O3	91.2	−1.2***	−0.4	0.1
O3 to O4	76.0	−2.6***	−1.9**	−0.4
O4 to O5	74.6	−4.3***	−4.6***	−3.8***
O5 to O6	46.9	−2.5	−7.7***	−4.1*
Retention as				
O1	99.8	0.1***	0.0	0.0
O2	99.3	0.0	−0.1	0.0
O3	70.1	4.8***	2.4***	5.4***
O4	87.9	1.7***	1.9**	4.4***
O5	81.4	2.5**	2.7	3.0**

NOTE: *** = statistically significant from zero at the 1 percent level; ** = statistically significant from zero at the 5 percent level; * = statistically significant from zero at the 10 percent level.

levels O3 and above. These results are consistent with earlier RAND research that found that black males were less likely to be promoted but more likely to be retained if promoted.

Overall, female officers are also less likely to be promoted than white males are (Table S.3). More specifically, female officers are less likely to be promoted to O2, O3, and O4 than white males are, with the exception that black women are about as likely to be promoted to O3 as white men are. Retention rates for female officers at O3 are also generally lower than those for males, with the exception that black women at O3 have a higher retention rate than white men. All women have lower retention rates than white men at O5, but, given retention, non-black women have higher promotion rates to O6 than men do. Across all grades, these results are roughly consistent with earlier RAND research that found lower retention and promotion rates for white women.

The combined effects of retention and promotion have varying effects on the likelihood of cohorts, as defined by race, sex, and Hispanic origin, reaching certain promotion and retention milestones (Table S.4). On net, white and Hispanic males have nearly identical likelihoods of reaching O4, while black and other minority men are more likely to reach O4. The lower likelihoods that black and Hispanic males have of promotion at each level through O4 are offset by their higher rates of retention. For Hispanic men, the effects are exactly offsetting. For black men, the retention effect more than offsets the promotion effect, so black men are more likely to reach O4. The results for black men differ from the earlier RAND research, which found that the effects were fully offsetting for black men, leaving black and white men equally likely to reach the rank of O4. With respect to their later careers, among O4 officers, black and Hispanic men are less likely to achieve O6 than white men are, with lower promotion rates more than offsetting higher retention rates. Other minority men have a higher likelihood of reaching

Table S.3
Estimated Percentage Point Differences in the Likelihood of Reaching Promotion and Retention Milestones for Female Officers

Milestone	Percentage of White Male Officers Retained/ Promoted	Percentage Point Difference: Minority Female Officers – White Male Officers			
		White Females	Black Females	Hispanic Females	Other Minority Females
Promotion					
O1 to O2	98.5	−0.8***	−1.5***	−1.8***	−0.9***
O2 to O3	91.2	−2.5***	−0.2	−1.8**	−1.7***
O3 to O4	76.0	−3.2***	−3.9***	−1.8	−3.7**
O4 to O5	74.6	0.6	−6.8***	−6.4	−3.3
O5 to O6	46.9	3.4**	−7.7**	13.1	16.6**
Retention as					
O1	99.8	0.0	−0.1	−0.3***	−0.2***
O2	99.3	−0.4***	−0.2*	0.2	−0.2
O3	70.1	−10.9***	4.2***	−4.7**	−3.7**
O4	87.9	−3.5***	−0.5	2.5	−0.4
O5	81.4	−10.9***	−5.7**	−9.6	−8.8*

NOTE: *** = statistically significant from zero at the 1 percent level; ** = statistically significant from zero at the 5 percent level; * = statistically significant from zero at the 10 percent level.

Table S.4
Likelihood of an Entry Cohort Reaching Promotion and Retention Milestones

	Percentage of Entering Officer Cohort Reaching:	
	O1 to O4 Promotion	O4 to O6 Promotion
Male officers		
White	45.4	23.6
Black	47.2***	19.5***
Hispanic	45.9	20.1
Other	48.4***	21.0
Female officers		
White	30.8***	18.8***
Black	45.3	15.6***
Hispanic	36.4***	23.1
Other	37.2***	26.8

NOTE: *** = statistically significant from white male officers at the 1 percent level;
** = statistically significant from white male officers at the 5 percent level;
* = statistically significant from white male officers at the 10 percent level.

O4 than white men have, but, once reaching O4, a slightly lower likelihood of reaching O6. However, only the result for black men is precisely estimated.

On net, female entrants are less likely to achieve O4 than their male counterparts, with the exception of black women. The lower likelihoods of achieving O4 stem from lower rates of both retention and promotion. Once they have achieved O4, white, black, and Hispanic female officers are less likely to achieve O6 than white males are, though only the differences for white and black women are statistically different from zero. Black women have an especially low likelihood of achieving O6, particularly because of their lower rates of retention at O5 and lower rates of promotion from O5 to O6. Other minority women, once they have achieved O4, are more likely to achieve promotion to O6 than any other group, including white males, particularly because of their higher rates of promotion from O5 to O6, though the difference from white males is not statistically different from zero.

Female Officer Career Progression in Restricted Occupations

To test whether occupational restrictions on female officers could account for any differences in their rates of retention and promotion, we compared career progress for women in occupations partially closed to them with that in occupations fully open to them, and netted out the differences for men in those same occupations. In general, we find no statistically significant difference in the likelihood of reaching O6, for women who have reached O4 (see Table S.5).

Table S.5
Percentage of Officers Reaching O6 in Open Versus Partially Closed Occupations, Conditional on Reaching O4

	Male Officers	Female Officers	Difference for Female Versus Male Officers
Open	22.9	18.9***	
Partially closed	24.6	19.2	
Net effect	1.7	0.3	–1.4

NOTE: *** Statistically significant from male officers at the 1 percent level; ** Statistically significant from male officers at the 5 percent level; * Statistically significant from male officers at the 10 percent level.

Unanswered Questions

Our work describes differences in officer career progression by race, sex, and Hispanic origin, as well as by whether occupations are partially closed to women. Our work updates and confirms some earlier findings. Nevertheless, there are some questions it does not answer.

First, it does not indicate whether recent officer cohorts will experience the same career progression as described here. This is because our data on career progression, especially in the more senior grades, are drawn from older cohorts who have had time to achieve high rank.

Second, our analysis does not indicate how lifting or reducing career restrictions on service by women affected their career progression. This is because the career progression in occupations open or partially closed to women may differ in important ways from that in fully closed ones. Model estimation and simulation of career progression under alternative policies that lift restrictions on service by women could shed some light here.

Third, our control variables do not control for myriad other possible contributors to differences in career progression by race, sex, and Hispanic origin, as indicated earlier. Some variables for which we do not control are ability and proficiencies, differences in performance and opportunities for command experience, access to mentors and peer networks, occupational choices more specific than those we analyze, and promotion selection criteria. Insofar as these vary by race, sex, and Hispanic origin, they could explain some of the differences we find in career progression.

Acknowledgments

We are grateful to the Defense Manpower Data Center (DMDC) for providing the Proxy-PERSTEMPO used in our analysis and to Teri Cholar at DMDC. We also benefited from comments we received from the Office of Officer and Enlisted Personnel Management (OEPM) and from the Office of Accession Policy (AP) within the Office of the Under Secretary of Defense for Personnel and Readiness (Military Personnel Policy). We would especially like to thank Lernes Hebert, the director of OEPM, and Curtis Gilroy, the director of AP and the sponsor of this research. We also would like to thank our project monitor, John Jessup, within AP. Our report benefited from comments we received from John Winkler and Susan Hosek. Susan Hosek, along with Larry Hanser, provided technical reviews of the report, and we wish to thank them for their helpful input. We would also like to thank Laura Miller and Jennifer Kavanaugh for information on the status of occupations currently partially open to women and for sharing information on their project on gender integration in the military. Finally, we would like to thank Arthur Bullock, who provided excellent programming support, and Clifford Grammich, who provided communication support.

Abbreviations

AP	Office of Accession Policy
BASD	base entry service date
DMDC	Defense Manpower Data Center
DoD	Department of Defense
FY	fiscal year
MLDC	Military Leadership Diversity Commission
MOS	military occupational specialty
OEPM	Office of Officer and Enlisted Personnel Management
ROTC	Reserve Officer Training Corps

CHAPTER ONE

Introduction

Our study was motivated by an ongoing concern within the Department of Defense (DoD) about the diversity of the military's leadership, especially in the more senior officer corps. The diversity of the officer corps has been the focus of several commissions, including the Fahy Committee in the late 1950s, the Gessell Committee in the early 1960s, and most recently the 2011 Military Leadership Diversity Commission (MLDC) (Department of Defense, 2011). Although the diversity of the officer corps has increased historically (Lim, Cho, and Curry, 2008), minority and female officers are less likely to be in the senior officer ranks (O4 through general and flag officer ranks) than in the junior officer ranks. Table 1.1 shows that in fiscal year (FY) 2009, the most recent year for which DoD has published data, female officers made up 17.96 percent of junior officers in the grades of O1 to O3, but 12.72 percent in grades O4 to O6 and 5.6 percent of general and flag officers.[1] While the percentages differ, the pattern is similar for racial minorities and Hispanics. Thus, officer diversity remains an ongoing concern.

Understanding the underrepresentation of minority and female officers in the senior ranks requires an understanding of differences in their career progression and the factors that affect those differences. *Career progression* refers to the process by which an individual becomes an officer, pursues his or her military career, and advances through the ranks. Differences in career progression may be due to a number of factors, including entry source and qualifica-

Table 1.1
Active Component Officer Corps, by Gender, Race, Ethnicity Status, FY 2009 (%)

Service	Accessions	O1 to O3	O4 to O6	General and Flag Officers	All Officers
Female	20.58	17.96	12.72	5.60	16.21
White	75.81	77.27	83.71	92.97	78.86
Black	9.19	8.90	8.13	5.82	8.74
Asian	4.93	4.01	2.53	0.44	3.74
Other, two or more, unknown	10.07	9.81	5.73	0.77	8.66
Hispanic	5.59	5.59	4.11	1.32	5.20

SOURCE: Department of Defense, 2011, Tables B-23, B-27, B-38, and B-39.

---

[1] In the appendix, we present additional tabulations on the demographics of different entry cohorts of officers.

tions, occupation and job assignment, retention behavior, promotion selection criteria, and performance.

Related to the issue of the underrepresentation of women in the senior officer ranks is the issue of restrictions on the service of women in the military.[2] Because women are prohibited from being assigned to units below the brigade level with a primary mission to be directly engaged in ground combat, they may be restricted from serving in assignments that lead to promotion. These restrictions may therefore limit their career progression to the senior ranks. A number of occupations are fully closed to women, and some are partially closed. By *partially closed*, we mean occupations that are deemed open but that have some positions for which assignment of women is restricted. A question of interest is whether the career progression of women in restricted occupations differs from progression in unrestricted occupations and whether lifting those restrictions might be expected to improve promotion and retention among women.

The research summarized in this report focuses on two aspects of the career progression process, promotion and retention, and focuses on officers only. It analyzes gender and minority differences in the attainment of successive promotion and retention milestones of entry cohorts of officers as they progress through their careers. It also analyzes differences in career progression among female officers in partially closed versus open ones. The approach we use identifies whether differences in officer career progression by minority status and gender and by occupational closure status are due to differences in promotion rates, retention rates, or both. It also uses regression methods to account for several factors that might explain gender, minority, and closure differences in career progression, such as service, broad occupational area, source of commission, entry year, prior service status, marital status, education, and deployment experience. Specifically, the study assesses differences in the fraction of

- officers promoted to successive grades, given they are retained at the previous grade, i.e., retained until their eligibility for promotion to that grade
- officers retained between promotion boards, i.e., the fraction of promoted officers who stay until they are eligible to be promoted to the next grade
- an entering cohort of officers that attains a particular career milestone.

This report summarizes our findings. The analysis is descriptive because it focuses on describing differences in career progression. While we net out some of the sources of differences through our regression methodology, the analysis does not indicate why the observed differences occur. Nonetheless, by describing differences using the most recently available data, it provides the most up-to-date look at where differences continue to occur.

Earlier RAND Study

The analysis of gender and minority career progression differences is an update of an earlier RAND study conducted in the mid-1990s and reported in Hosek et al. (2001). The study

---

[2]   Several RAND studies have examined assignment of women in the military and gender integration, including Harrell et al. (2007, 2002) and Harrell and Miller (1997). A companion report to this one is examining progress in the assignment of women (Miller et al., forthcoming). These reports describe the history of assignment policy for women in the military and provide analysis of progress in terms of gender integration.

was used to support the findings of the 1999 report by the Office of the Under Secretary of Defense for Personnel and Readiness on the career progression of minority and female officers (Department of Defense, 1999). The earlier RAND report tracked the retention and promotion outcomes of active-duty officers (excluding those in the medical and professional fields) who entered the officer ranks between 1967 through 1991 through the grade of O6. These outcomes were tracked using data from 1977 through 1994, and the authors compared the outcomes of minority and female officers with those of white male officers, accounting for differences in service, occupational group, commissioning source, entry year, and prior service. To better understand why differences occurred among groups and to understand the services' career pipelines better, the authors also conducted interviews of career managers and focus groups of officers and members of promotion boards. Because the analysis reported in this document seeks to update the earlier RAND study, we provide an overview of its key findings.

The earlier RAND study found that, accounting for other factors, relative to white male officers, promotion rates for white women were slightly lower in the junior ranks and higher at the field grade level (O4), but white women left at earlier career stages. On net, entering white female officers were less likely to achieve O4. Promotion rates for black female officers were lower than for white male officers at all levels, but black women were no less likely to leave early in their careers. About as many black as white female officers reached the O4 promotion point, a figure substantially less than that for white male officers. Black male officers generally failed promotion at higher rates than white male officers, but black men who were promoted were more likely to stay in service. The effects were offsetting, so that, on net, black and white male entrants had the same likelihood of reaching the rank of O4, and men were more likely than women to make it to O4. The study also considered career progression to O6, but small sample sizes for certain groups, specifically minority women, prevented the researchers from drawing conclusions about this stage of the officer career. The study considered the promotion and retention results of other minority groups, but the findings were limited due to small sample sizes.

The earlier RAND study also conducted extensive focus groups and interviews. The results indicated that (1) black officers had greater difficulty forming peer and mentor relationships that are considered key elements of a successful career and (2) more frequent assignments to Reserve Officer Training Corps (ROTC) and recruiting have the effect of pulling black officers out of the assignments that are typical for their occupations. The study found that women perceive limited occupational roles and have concerns about harassment issues and about balancing family obligations.

The analysis in the earlier report is also relevant to the recent assessment of military leadership diversity conducted by the congressionally mandated MLDC, which sought to assess the policies and practices that shape diversity among military leaders. The MLDC considered an array of factors that affect the career life cycles of military personnel and concluded that minority and female officers were underrepresented among initial officer accessions, had lower representation in career fields associated with promotion, and had lower promotion rates. It also found that mid-level women had lower retention.

However, because the MLDC conducted its deliberations within a short time frame, it was not able to conduct an analysis that tracked the career progression of entry officer cohorts over time and accounted for factors other than gender and minority status that could explain differences in career progression. Such information is useful because it helps to better pinpoint whether differences in career progression are present after accounting for some of the factors that could explain the differences. It is also useful to better understand how the career progression of women differs depending on whether they are in open or partially closed occupations. The current study fills this gap.[3]

Changes Since the Earlier RAND Study

Much has changed since the late 1990s, and it is unclear whether the earlier study results remain relevant. Some of these changes have affected the management of all officers, not specifically minority and female officers, and it is unclear whether there are differential effects for minority and female officers. For example, the drawdown of military forces in the 1990s at the end of the Cold War, and the methods the services used to accomplish the drawdown, reduced retention and changed promotion opportunities (Congressional Budget Office, 1999). Similarly, the attacks of September 11, 2001, and the subsequent military operations in Iraq and Afghanistan changed perceptions about military service. Analysis of deployment and officer retention indicates that increasing amounts of deployment are associated with greater officer retention (Fricker, 2002). An additional factor is the increase in military pay and benefits. During the 1990s, military pay raises did not keep pace with private-sector pay, leading to recruiting and retention shortfalls (Asch, Hosek, and Warner, 2001). In 2000, Congress authorized pay raises through 2006 that were higher than changes in civilian pay, as well as increases in the housing allowance. These compensation produced an increase in retention (Asch, Hosek, and Warner, 2001). Other force management changes have occurred since the 1990s, such as downsizing by the Navy.

Demographic and economic factors in the United States at large have also changed. For example, growth in the Hispanic population accounted for most of the growth in the U.S. population between 2000 and 2010, potentially affecting the pool of officer applicants (Passel, Cohn, and Lopez, 2011). Trends in the civilian pay opportunities of officers are less clear, but some information can be gained by considering the trends in the growth of civilian wages of college graduates relative to high school graduates—the so-called college wage premium. This trend is relevant because officers have at least a four-year college degree. Analysis of the college wage premium shows steady growth through 2006 for both men and women since the early 1980s (Hubbard, 2009). Analysis also shows steady growth for black and Hispanic men and women, though the trends show year-to-year variation. Furthermore, growth between 2000 and 2006 was less discernible for all groups, except for men, for whom growth has been steady. Past research shows that changes in military pay relative to civilian pay affect retention (Hansen and Wenger, 2002).

The final area of change since the 1990s has been the services' efforts to improve officer diversity. While a complete inventory of diversity programs is beyond the scope of this research, the services have a variety of efforts underway to address diversity. These are summarized by Lim, Cho, and Curry (2008).

There is no previous quantitative study of the career progression of female officers in open versus partially closed occupations in the military. Harrell et al. (2002) considered the status of gender integration in a selected set of occupations, including several officer occupations, but

---

[3] One other recent study has assessed minority and gender differences in officer career progression, and the factors affecting these differences. However, the study focused only on the Air Force, and its results are not publicly available.

the occupations they considered for officers were closed to women, preventing comparisons of the career progression milestones of women in restricted occupations with those in unrestricted ones.

The MLDC conducted a review of the policies and practices that shape diversity of military leaders. Among the recommendations in its 2011 report (Military Leadership Diversity Commission, 2011) was one to eliminate the "combat exclusion" policy for women. The 2011 National Defense Authorization Act (Pub. L. 111-383) requires that the Secretary of Defense review the policies, laws, and regulations that restrict the service of female members of the armed service. DoD is currently conducting that review.

Given the changes that have occurred and questions about the relevance of the earlier work, the Director of Accession Policy within the Office of the Under Secretary of Defense for Personnel and Readiness asked RAND to update the earlier study of race/ethnicity and gender differences in promotion and retention to ascertain whether and how these differences have changed relative to the earlier study's findings. Furthermore, as part of its deliberations on restrictions on the service of female members, the Director of Accession Policy also asked RAND to provide information on the career progression of women in partially closed occupations, i.e., those that have positions for which service by women is restricted. This report summarizes our findings.

Organization of This Report

The next chapter presents more information about the data we used, how we define race and ethnicity, and how we identify partially closed occupations. It also briefly describes our approach for determining retention and promotion outcomes, with more details provided in the appendix. Chapter Three presents our results on differences in the retention and promotion of minority and female officers. Chapter Four presents our results on differences in the retention and promotion of female officers in partially closed versus open occupations, relative to the differences for male officers. Chapter Five summarizes our findings and conclusions.

CHAPTER TWO

Overview of Data and Approach

Our analysis focuses on career progression for all services through the grade of O6. This chapter presents an overview of our data and methodology. More details about the construction of our analysis file, as well as regression results, are in the appendix. We begin with an overview of the input data, the retention and promotion milestones we consider, how we measure retention and promotion in the data, and entry cohorts we use for measuring each milestone. We then discuss our approach to estimating differences in career progression. We discuss how we define race and ethnicity in our analysis, how we identify occupations partially closed to women, and the variables we consider in our analysis.

Data

We use the Proxy-PERSTEMPO data file maintained by the Defense Manpower Data (DMDC) as our input data. The file contains longitudinal administrative records on active-duty personnel by month from January 1993 through September 2010 and for the last month in each quarter going back to January 1988.[1] The data include a snapshot of everyone on active duty in a given month or quarter and track them until they separate from active duty or until the end of the file in 2010. For officers, the data include service; occupation (using the DoD occupational coding); grade; months of service before attaining current grade; source of commission; date of entry and date of commissioning; demographic information, including race, ethnicity, gender, marital status, and education; and indicators of deployment based on receipt of two deployment-related pays, family separation pay, and hostile fire pay.[2] Because the data indicate both date of entry into the military and date of commissioning, we are able to ascertain whether an officer has enlisted service prior to becoming an officer.

Using these monthly and quarterly data, we are able to ascertain for all officers in the data their entry path in terms of commissioning source and prior service, their promotion path, and whether and when they left active duty. We use this information to construct the career progression of each officer in terms of retention and promotion, as described in the next subsection.

---

[1] The file actually begins October 1987, but our analysis relies on data beginning January 1988.

[2] The approach used to measure deployment with these pay elements, and their drawbacks, is discussed at length in Hosek and Totten (1998).

Because our focus is on the career progression of officers, we exclude officers who do not enter the officer ranks at the grade of O1.[3] This has the effect of deleting from the analysis officers principally in professional occupations, such as medical, legal, and religious career fields. The approach is consistent with the earlier RAND study, though it had the effect in the earlier study of eliminating occupations with substantial proportions of female officers, and presumably this is the case in our data as well. These officers are put into a separate competitive category for promotion, so their career paths are not consistent with the other officers we study.

Defining Retention and Promotion Milestones

As in the earlier RAND study, we measure career progression in this study as a series of retention and promotion milestones, each conditional on its predecessor. The milestones are listed in the second column of Table 2.1. Thus, for example, we analyze promotion to O3 only for officers who stayed as an O1 until eligible for promotion to O2, were promoted to O2, and stayed as an O2 until eligible for promotion to O3. We analyze each milestone separately, and the analysis includes all officers who reached that milestone. Thus, an officer who left as an O2 before reaching eligibility for promotion to O3 would not be included in the analysis of promotion to O3. Retention is measured conditional on achieving the previous grade (except O1, where it is conditional on officer commissioning), and retention is measured up to the point of eligibility for the next promotion. For example, retention as an O3 is measured for those who achieved O2 and includes retention until the beginning of the promotion window to O3. Thus, retention milestones are retention between promotion boards. We discuss later in this section and in the appendix how we define retention milestones and promotion eligibility.

Table 2.1
Career Progression Milestones and Cohorts Used in the Analysis

Career Milestone Number	Career Milestone	Entering Cohorts Used
1	Retained as O1	1988–2002
2	Promoted to O2	1988–2002
3	Retained as O2	1986–2002
4	Promoted to O3	1986–2002
5	Retained as O3	1983–2002
6	Promoted to O4	1983–1999
7	Retained as O4	1977–1993
8	Promoted to O5	1977–1993
9	Retained as O5	1971–1991
10	Promoted to O6	1971–1991

---

[3] We can be sure we eliminate these officers only for the post-1988 cohorts. For pre-1988 cohorts, we do not observe entry as O1, so we match officers to a cohort based on the first observed promotion. These cohorts may include officers who entered after O1.

Since our data are for the period 1988 through 2010, they cover different periods of service for different entering cohorts of officers. For those who entered on or after 1988, the data cover their entire active-duty career until separation or until 2010. For those who entered active duty before 1988, we observe only the portion of their active-duty career that occurs during or after 1988. The result is that the promotion and retention milestones are measured with different subsets of entering cohorts.

The right column of Table 2.1 shows which entering cohorts are used for each milestone. The table shows that early career milestones are measured using recent entry cohorts. For example, retention as an O1 and promotion to O2 are measured using cohorts of officers that were commissioned between 1988 and 2002. Retention as an O2 and promotion to O3 are measured using cohorts that entered as early as 1986 and as late as 2002. In contrast, the later career milestones are measured using older entry cohorts. The most recent entry cohort used to measure retention as an O5 and promotion to O6 is the 1991 cohort, and the oldest cohort is the 1971 cohort. That is, the last cohort for which we can observe promotion to O6 is the 1991 cohort, and the earliest one is 1971.

Our entry cohorts overlap the entry cohorts used in the earlier RAND study. That study used cohorts as early as 1967 and as late as 1991. Thus, the cohorts in the earlier study are generally older, but there is overlap for the 1971 through 1991 cohorts. Our study tracks personnel through 2010, whereas the earlier study tracked them through 1994.

Because analysis of early career milestones is based on younger entry cohorts and analysis of later milestones is based on older cohorts, the results we observe regarding minority and gender differences in career progression may be due to differences in the behavior and performance of officers and the management policies and practices that influence their careers that are relevant across cohorts, and not to the effect of current policies governing career progression or diversity. That is, the analysis does not identify the effects that current policies could have on the future career progression of recent entry cohorts.

Determining promotion milestones in DMDC data, including the Proxy-PERSTEMPO data, is challenging because the data do not indicate who was considered eligible for promotion. As noted earlier, we assess promotion in our analysis only for those who have been retained to the beginning of the promotion eligibility window. Thus, determining promotion eligibility is essential for our analysis. Following the earlier RAND study, we identified a three-year promotion eligibility window for each grade, cohort, and service based on observed promotions in the data. In general, for each grade, cohort, and service, we identified the six-month period when at least 95 percent of all promotions occurred. This six-month period was then designated as the center of the promotion window for that grade, cohort, and service, and we added 15 months prior to this period and 15 months after this period, for a total of 36 months. For our study, a promotion is considered to have occurred only if an officer eligible for promotion achieves promotion to the next grade during these promotion eligibility windows. If the officer was promoted after the window, he or she is considered not promoted.

We define retention milestones in the context of our promotion window definitions. Retention is defined as staying until at least the first month of the promotion window. For example, retention as an O3 is defined to include all officers in an entry cohort and service who achieved O3 and who stayed in service at least until the first month of the promotion eligibility window for O4 for that cohort/service. Because the time until the next promotion window varies with grade, the length of retention windows will vary with grade, cohort, and service. For example, it takes about four years for an O2 to achieve an O3 promotion and about six years for an O3 to achieve an O4 promotion. Thus, the O3 retention window will be longer than the O2 window.

If the end of the data in 2010 occurred prior to the end of the 36-month window or the end of a retention window, we excluded the grade/cohort/service combinations from the analysis. Thus, the analysis is conducted only on data for which we have complete windows. Similarly, we include only those grade/cohort/service combinations for which we had complete windows for cohorts that entered prior to 1988. For example, for officers who were an O2 when we first observe them in 1988, we include only the portion of their career beginning when they become an O3 because we do not observe their complete duration as an O1 or O2.

We summarize the data by computing the percentage of officers reaching each career progression milestone in our data, averaging across all cohorts and services. These tabulations are shown in Table 2.2. For comparison's sake, we also show the corresponding percentages from the earlier RAND study.

Considering promotion first, we find that average promotion rates are slightly higher than in the earlier study for each promotion through O5, but the promotion rate to O6 is lower.

Table 2.2
Percentage of Officers Retained/Promoted in Updated Analysis and Earlier RAND Study

Milestone	Updated Analysis	Earlier RAND Study[a]
Promotion:		
O1 to O2	97.3	95.3
O2 to O3	90.8	87.9
O3 to O4	76.1	74.6
O4 to O5	74.6	73.6
O5 to O6	46.4	50.2
Retention as:		
O1	99.8	100.0
O2	99.3	92.1
O3	70.3	64.6
O4	88.5	89.3
O5	80.3	68.5
Combined attainment:		
O1 through O4 promotion	46.9	37.9
O4 through O6 promotion	24.6	15.4

SOURCE: Updated analysis is based on authors' calculations. Earlier RAND study results are from Hosek et al. (2001).

[a] The earlier RAND study could not separately distinguish retention as O1 and promotion to O2, so these milestones were combined in that study. The average percentage of officers in that study that were retained as O1 and promoted to O2 was 95.3 percent. In this table, we indicate this percentage as the percentage that promote to O2 and arbitrarily designate the percentage who retain as O1 as 100 percent.

For example, in our updated study we find that 76.1 percent of those eligible for promotion to O4 are promoted, while the earlier study found a figure of 74.6 percent. However, we find that 46.4 percent of eligible officers are promoted to O5, compared with 50.2 percent in the earlier study.

On the other hand, we find that retention is generally higher in our updated analysis, on average. Retention among those who have been promoted to O2 is 99.3 percent in our analysis, compared with 92.1 percent in the earlier analysis. We find that 70.3 percent of O3s who have been promoted stay until they are eligible to be promoted to O4, compared with 64.6 percent in the earlier study. The exception is retention as an O4. We find about the same retention at this career milestone, 88.5 percent, relative to the 89.3 percent figure found in the earlier study. However, we find that 80.3 percent of those who had been promoted to O5 stay until they are eligible for an O6 promotion, compared with 68.5 percent in the earlier study.

Putting the promotion and retention information together, we can compute the average percentage of entry officers who attain an O4 promotion, and the percentage who attain an O6 promotion, given they reached O4. These figures are shown at the bottom of Table 2.2. We find that 46.9 percent of officers in the updated analysis reach O4, compared with 37.9 percent in the earlier study. The higher percentage in the updated analysis is primarily due to higher retention. We also find that a higher percentage reach O6 in the updated analysis, 24.6 percent compared with 15.4 percent, despite the fact that we find a lower percentage of officers achieving O6 given they were eligible. This higher percentage is attributable to the higher average retention past 20 years when the officers were O5.

Approach for Estimating Differences and for Defining Key Variables

For each of the career milestones in Table 2.1, we estimate the difference in the likelihood of reaching that milestone by minority and gender status, holding constant the other factors that we describe below. We estimate separate regressions for each milestone, and we estimate the likelihood of reaching a given milestone conditional on having reached the previous one. Thus, the regression for the likelihood of being retained as an O2 is conditional on having been promoted to O2.

We estimate probit regressions and present the full results for all covariates in the appendix. In Chapters Three and Four, we report the marginal effects of the key variables. In Chapter Three, the key variables are the dummy variables on race, ethnicity, and gender. In Chapter Four, the key variables are those indicating whether a female officer is in a partially closed occupation. The marginal effect gives the change in the likelihood of reaching the milestone for a discrete change in the dummy variable from 0 to 1.

More formally, in Chapter Three, the probit regression to estimate gender and minority differences in career progression is of the form

$$\Pr\left(outcome_j = 1\right) = F\left(D_i\delta + X_i\beta\right), \tag{1}$$

where i indicates individual officer i, j indicates each of the ten promotion and retention outcomes in Table 2.1, D_i is a set of dummy variables for each race, ethnicity, and gender group for individual i, X_i is a set of control variables, and δ and β are coefficients that we seek to estimate. We report the marginal effects of race, ethnicity, and gender, given by

$$F\left(D_i = 1 \mid \bar{X}_i \hat{\beta}\right) - F\left(D_i = 0 \mid \bar{X}_i \hat{\beta}\right). \tag{2}$$

It is important to recognize that this regression analysis is descriptive in nature. Our objective is not to explain the factors affecting the promotion or retention of officers or to explain how being a minority or a female officer affects career progression. The regression analysis only describes the extent of career progression differences by gender, race, and ethnicity, controlling for some of the factors that affect promotion and retention. Not all factors that might affect retention or promotion are included, such as metrics of personnel quality, for example. Some of these omitted factors are known to be correlated with race, ethnicity, or gender and affect the regression estimates of minority and gender status. Thus, importantly, we cannot interpret the coefficient estimates on minority or gender status as the effect that being a minority or a female officer has on career progression. Furthermore, because our objective is not to explain retention or promotion outcomes, we do not attempt to explain how promotion outcomes may affect retention and vice versa.[4]

In Chapter Four, we seek to estimate the difference in the likelihood of achieving each outcome for women in occupations partially closed to women versus those that are open. A simple comparison of outcomes for women in restricted occupations versus those for women in open occupations is problematic, however, because the observed differences might be due to occupation-specific differences and not due to differences for women, per se. That is, we need a control comparison that accounts for differences in outcomes for partially closed occupations versus open ones, irrespective of whether those occupations are filled by women. Our analysis uses differences in outcomes for men in partially closed occupations versus occupations as a control. That is, we estimate the difference in career progression for women in partially closed versus open occupations net of the difference for men. This approach is a type of "difference-in-difference" approach, because we consider female-male differences in partially closed versus open occupations.[5] Our analysis deletes occupations that are fully closed to women, and hence are filled only by men. Thus, our comparisons of career progression for women versus men only compare occupations that are partially closed to those fully open.

More specifically, the probit we estimate is of the form

$$\Pr\left(outcome_j = 1\right) = F\left(\alpha_1 P + \alpha_2 G + \alpha_3 \left(P \times G\right) + X_i \beta\right), \tag{3}$$

where P is a dummy variable indicating whether the officer is in an occupation that is partially closed to women, G is a dummy variable indicating that the officer is female, $P \times G$ is a dummy variable indicating that the officer is a female in a partially closed occupation, and α_1, α_2, and α_3 are coefficients that we seek to estimate. Later in this subsection we describe how we identify partially closed occupations. The coefficient α_1 captures differences in the probability of achieving different outcomes between occupations that partially are closed to women and open

---

[4]   Past studies have considered the effect of promotion timing on retention and how the retention decision might affect promotion (Buddin et al., 1992).

[5]   However, unlike typical difference-in-difference analysis, we do not seek to estimate the causal effect of the variable of interest, which in our case is the variable indicating whether a female officer is in a partially closed occupation.

occupations, regardless of whether the officer is male or female. The coefficient α_2 captures differences between female and male officers in the probability of achieving outcome j, regardless of occupation. The coefficient α_3 is the one of interest because it captures the difference-in-difference effect. We report the marginal effect of $P \times G$ in Chapter Four, given by

$$F\left((P \times G) = 1 \mid \bar{X}_i \hat{\beta}\right) - F\left((P \times G) = 0 \mid \bar{X}_i \hat{\beta}\right). \tag{4}$$

We considered alternative specifications to equation 3. In preliminary analysis, we tried using dummy variables for each individual race, ethnicity, and gender group separately rather than just considering women versus men without concern for race or ethnicity. We also tried using separate dummy variables for each partially closed individually rather than as a group. These alternative specifications suffered from the problem of limited sample size for individual demographic groups and for individual occupations. So, we considered all female officers as a group and we considered all partially closed occupations as a group. Thus, unlike in the previous analyses, we do not ascertain differences among women by race and ethnicity.

It is important to recognize that our approach prevents us from interpreting the findings as the causal effect of restrictions on the service by women on career progression outcomes. To interpret the estimates as the causal effect of partially opening occupations, we must assume, possibly incorrectly, that conditional on our control variables, the experience of men in these occupations is the correct counterfactual for women. That is, we must implicitly assume that had these occupations not been restricted, occupational differences for women in career progression would be the same as the differences for men with similar characteristics. This is highly unlikely if women evaluate their career options differently, if women make different retention decisions, if promotion criteria for women differ from those of men, and/or if men and women perform differently. More broadly, there may be other factors that cause outcomes to differ between male and female officers, other than whether the occupation is restricted to women, that are not controlled for among our control variables. Because of these limitations, our results can be considered only descriptions of how career progression for women differs in partially closed versus open occupations, net of the difference for men. They cannot be considered as estimates of how partially closed occupations have affected the career progression of female officers. We discuss an approach for estimating the causal effect in Chapter Five.

Approach for Estimating the Probability That Officers Progress Through Several Milestones
In addition to estimating differences in the probability of reaching each of the ten milestones, conditional on reaching the previous one, we also consider differences in the probability that an officer progresses through several milestones. To estimate the probability of progressing through several milestones, we use data for cohorts of officers where we observe them for a long enough period. We estimate separately the probability that entering officers attain O4 and the probability that officers who attained O4 also reached O6. The regressions control for other factors, and we report the results in the appendix.

Defining Race and Ethnicity
In the probit regressions in Chapter Three, we estimate differences between white males (the reference group) and up to seven other race/ethnicity/gender groups, depending on sample sizes: black male, Hispanic male, other minority male, white female, black female, Hispanic

female, and other minority female. A government-wide change occurred in January 2003 in how race and ethnicity are categorized, allowing a survey respondent to designate multiple races and to designate ethnicity separately (White House, 2000). However, our analysis uses the pre-2003 definitions of race and ethnicity because we consider only those officer cohorts that entered through 2002, and we define race and ethnicity based on the race and ethnicity designated at entry. Thus, an officer who entered in 2002 and stayed through 2006 would have his or her race and ethnicity defined using information from 2002.

The pre-2003 definition of race and ethnicity in the Proxy-PERSTEMPO data is based on a single variable that can take seven values: unknown, white, black, Hispanic, American Indian/Alaskan Native, Asian/Pacific Islander, or other. Limited sample size prevents us from considering each group separately in our analysis. We therefore consider the following groups: white, black, Hispanic, and other minority, where our definition of "other minority" includes American Indian/Alaskan Native, Asian/Pacific Islander, and other, as well as the unknown category.

Since we also analyze each race and ethnicity group separately by gender, the sample sizes in some cases are still small, even with our broad definition of the "other" category. Consequently, we are unable to draw inferences about differences in some cases, especially in the upper grades, because limited sample size leads to differences that are not statistically significant, even when the magnitude of the differences is large.

Identifying Occupations Partially Closed to Women

A companion report to our study is providing analysis in support of DoD's review of the laws, policies, and regulations that restrict the service of female members (Miller et al., forthcoming). As part of its effort, the study obtained from each service a list of occupations that are considered open as of 2011, but have some positions that are closed and unavailable to women. We call these occupations "partially closed." The list is the most up-to-date version and is included in the companion report. We incorporated the list into our analysis. Most of the occupations on the list are almost completely open, except for just a few positions. Consequently, tabulations in the companion report of FY 2011 authorizations in these occupations show that over 98 percent of positions are open to women. In contrast, a smaller subset of the occupations on the list is less than 98 percent open. We defined an occupation as partially closed to female officers if less than 98 percent of authorizations are open. Put differently, we considered an occupation as fully open if at least 98 percent of positions are open.[6] The occupations that are less than 98 percent open are listed in Table 2.3. For the most part, the occupations on the

---

[6] Thus, our analysis distinguishes between two groups, partially closed (<98 percent open) and fully open (≥98 percent open). We conducted three types of sensitivity analyses. We redid the regression analysis where we instead designated occupations into three groups: partially closed (<98 percent open), almost open (at least 98 percent but less than 100 percent open), and fully open (100 percent open). We found no difference in our results for the occupations designated partially closed. For the second sensitivity analysis, we redid the regressions where we used, instead, a variable to indicate the extent of closure rather than a dummy variable for whether the occupation is partially closed (<98 percent). The variable indicating extent of closure is not a continuous monotonic variable but tended to cluster at nearly 100 percent (between 98 and 100 percent) or between 75 and 90 percent, though there were a couple that were in the 30 percent range. The results are qualitatively similar to what we report in Chapter Five. We chose to use the dummy variable approach instead because of the tendency toward bimodal clustering. Finally, because the cutoff of 98 percent was arbitrarily chosen, we conducted a third sensitivity analysis to determine whether the results changed if we used other cutoff points (specifically, 99 percent and 96 percent). We found little change in our results qualitatively.

Table 2.3
Occupations Identified as Partially Closed to Women (with less than 98 percent of authorizations open)

Service Occupation	Title
Air Force 15W	Weather
Army 02A	Combat Arms Generalist
Army 02B	Infantry/Armor
Army 12A	Combat Engineer
Army 13A	Field Artillery, General
Army 15B	Aviation Combined Arms Operations
Army 25A	Signal, General
Army 31A	Military Police
Army 35D	All Source Intelligence
Army 38A	Civil Affairs
Army 42B	Human Resources Officer
Army 51R	Systems Automation Acquisition and Engineering
Army 74A	Chemical, Biological, Radiological, and Nuclear
Army 90A	Logistics
Marine Corps 0180	Adjunct: Personnel and Administration
Marine Corps 0202	Marine Air/Ground Task Force Intelligence Officer
Marine Corps 0402	Logistics Officer
Marine Corps 0530	Civil Affairs Officer
Marine Corps 0602	Communications Officer
Marine Corps 1302	Combat Engineer Officer
Marine Corps 2102	Ordnance Officer
Marine Corps 3002	Ground Supply Officer
Marine Corps 8041	Colonel, Ground
Navy 112X	Unrestricted Line Officer, Submarine Qualified
Navy 310X	Supply Corps Officer
Navy 6120	Limited Duty, Operations (Surface)
Navy 6400	Limited Duty Officer, Nuclear Power
Navy 6510	Limited Duty Officer, Supply Corps
Navy 7120	Operations Technician (Surface)

SOURCE: Derived from Miller et al. (forthcoming).

NOTE: List excludes professional occupations, including medical, chaplain, and legal.

list are closed in positions that are below the division level in ground-combat elements but are open at the brigade level or higher.

As mentioned, our approach requires that we exclude occupations that are closed and filled by men. We identified these closed occupations from Miller et al. (forthcoming), which also lists all occupations currently closed to women.

To determine whether an officer was in a partially closed occupation, we considered occupation designation as an O3. Preliminary tabulations indicated that not all officers, especially those in the Marine Corps, have an occupational designation in our data at entry or even as an O2. Therefore, our analysis of career progression differences among occupations is conditional on achieving the rank of O3, and consequently, we can present results only for career milestones beyond promotion to O3. Specifically, we present results for outcomes 5 through 10 in Table 2.1.

Control Variables

The control variables in the regressions allow us to separate the effects of race, ethnicity, gender, and, in the case of occupation restrictions, occupation from the effects of other factors that can influence career progression. We are not able to control for all factors that can influence career progression, such as performance, behavior, and physical fitness, because we lack data on these factors. Furthermore, while we control for broad occupational group categories, we do not control for individual occupation within each group in our analysis of minority and gender career progression differences. Thus, to the extent that there are promotion and retention differences across more narrowly defined occupations within an occupational group, our control variables will not account for these differences in estimating minority and gender differences. Still, the factors we include are a partial set of controls. The variables we included are service, source of commission, prior enlisted service, occupation group, deployment experience, marital status, and education. Because we use a different data source and over a different time period, we are able to include covariates that were not included in the earlier RAND study, notably marital status,[7] education, and deployment experience.

Some of these variables, notably marital status, education, occupational group, and deployment experience, can vary over an officer's career. For example, an officer who changes career fields will have different occupations over his or her career. We address this issue by defining these variables as of the time of the career milestone.[8] Thus, if an officer changes occupations as an O3, we use the original designation for career milestones through promotion to O3 and the new designation for later career milestones beginning with retention as an O3. Similarly, we define deployment experience as cumulative months of deployment, and we

---

[7]   The earlier study was interested in considering the effect of marital status on retention, especially for female officers, but did not include marital status in its regression analysis because marital status may not be independent from retention. Because our analysis is not concerned with explaining how marital status affects retention, but only with describing differences in outcomes after including control variables, we opted to include marital status, as well as education, in our regression analysis.

[8]   Note that this is true only for how we define broad occupational area and not the specific occupations partially closed to women. As discussed earlier in this chapter, we identify these occupations based on the officer's designation as an O3. In contrast, we identify broad occupational area dynamically based on the officer's designation at the time of the career milestone.

define deployment as receiving family separation pay and/or hostile fire pay. The number of cumulative months is based on total months as of the career milestone under consideration. Thus, for analysis of promotion to O3, we count months of deployment up until eligibility for O3 promotion.

In a similar fashion, because marital status and education can vary over the career, we consider marital status and education status at each milestone. Thus, if marital status changed, for example, the new marital status would be considered at the relevant career milestones when status changed. That said, the information we use is only as good as the Proxy-PERSTEMPO data. Insofar as education and marital status are not updated in these data as they change over a member's career, their values will not change and we will not capture those changes in our analysis. We conducted sensitivity analysis and used entry-level education and marital status in our regressions for each milestone, and we found that our results regarding minority and gender differences in career progression were unchanged if we used entry-level education and marital status rather than status at the time of the milestone. We also examined the effect of omitting education and marital status. We generally found that the estimated minority and gender differences in career progression were either unchanged or slightly smaller than when we include these variables, but our overall conclusions are unchanged. We present results with these variables included.

In our analysis, we do not interact the control variables with the race/ethnicity/gender variables. Thus, we do not capture whether the effects of race/ethnicity/gender vary depending on the value of these variables. Tabulations of these variables show some variation with race/ethnicity and gender, as we show in tables in the appendix. Because the definition of race and ethnicity changed in 2003, we cannot compare characteristics of cohorts that entered before and after 2003. In the appendix, we show tabulations for pre-2003 cohorts and for officers in our analysis file (i.e., we exclude those in the professional fields).

Of particular note is that we do not interact marital status with the race/ethnicity/gender variables. While we control for marital status overall, we do not capture how gender differences, for example, vary depending on marital status. In part, this is because we have limited sample sizes for minority women, so cutting the data even more by marital status was not feasible.

CHAPTER THREE

Results on Minority and Gender Differences in Career Progression

This chapter summarizes our results on the career progression of minority and female officers relative to white male officers. We report the regression results in the appendix. In this chapter, we first show estimated differences in career progression at each retention and promotion milestone, conditional on achieving the previous milestone. These results tell us whether differences in career progression by minority and gender status occur because of differences in promotion outcomes, differences in retention outcomes, or both, and at which specific milestones the differences occur. We then consider differences by race, ethnicity, and gender in the likelihood an entry officer reaches each career milestone. This analysis puts the conditional retention and promotion results together to allow us to discern the joint effect of differences in retention and promotion. Again, we caution the reader to recall that while the analysis provides a description of career progression differences, we cannot draw conclusions about whether minorities or female officers with the same characteristics as white male officers experience different career progression because we do not control for every factor that might affect differences in career progression. If we could control for every relevant factor, the observed differences reported here could disappear.

Conditional Differences in Achieving Career Milestones

Table 3.1 shows the estimated differences in the likelihood of achieving each career milestone, conditional on achieving the previous milestone, for male officers. Table 3.2 shows the estimated differences for female officers. The differences are measured relative to white males, our comparison group, and we show the percentage of white males reaching each career milestone, conditional on achieving the previous one, in the left part of each table. The left-hand side of each table shows the estimated percentage point difference in the likelihood of reaching a given milestone for minority male officers (in Table 3.1) and for female officers (in Table 3.2) relative to white males. For example, the −1.1 estimate for black males in Table 3.1 means that, controlling for other factors, the percentage of O1 black men who are promoted to O2 is 1.1 percentage points less than the percentage of O1 white men.

Generally, we find that minority men are less likely to be promoted but are more likely to be retained, given they were promoted, than white men. The results differ in magnitude and statistical significance for different minority groups and career milestones. Furthermore, the differences between white and minority male officers occur primarily in the field grades of O3 to O6, especially during the retention windows.

Table 3.1
Estimated Percentage Point Differences in the Likelihood of Reaching Promotion and Retention Milestones for Male Officers

Milestone	Percentage of White Male Officers Retained/ Promoted	Percentage Point Difference: Minority Male Officers – White Male Officers		
		Black Males	Hispanic Males	Other Minority Males
Promotion				
O1 to O2	98.5	−1.1***	−0.5***	−0.1
O2 to O3	91.2	−1.2***	−0.4	0.1
O3 to O4	76.0	−2.6***	−1.9**	−0.4
O4 to O5	74.6	−4.3***	−4.6***	−3.8***
O5 to O6	46.9	−2.5	−7.7***	−4.1*
Retention as				
O1	99.8	0.1***	0.0	0.0
O2	99.3	0.0	−0.1	0 0
O3	70.1	4.8***	2.4***	5.4***
O4	87.9	1.7***	1.9**	4.4***
O5	81.4	2.5**	2.7	3.0**

NOTE: *** = statistically significant from zero at the 1 percent level; ** = statistically significant from zero at the 5 percent level; * = statistically significant from zero at the 10 percent level.

Table 3.2
Estimated Percentage Point Differences in the Likelihood of Reaching Promotion and Retention Milestones for Female Officers

Milestone	Percentage of White Male Officers Retained/ Promoted	Percentage Point Difference: Minority Female Officers – White Male Officers			
		White Females	Black Females	Hispanic Females	Other Minority Females
Promotion					
O1 to O2	98.5	−0.8***	−1.5***	−1.8***	−0.9***
O2 to O3	91.2	−2.5***	−0.2	−1.8**	−1.7***
O3 to O4	76.0	−3.2***	−3.9***	−1.8	−3.7**
O4 to O5	74.6	0.6	−6.8***	−6.4	−3.3
O5 to O6	46.9	3.4**	−7.7**	13.1	16.6**
Retention as					
O1	99.8	0.0	−0.1	−0.3***	−0.2***
O2	99.3	−0.4***	−0.2*	0.2	−0.2
O3	70.1	−10.9***	4.2***	−4.7**	−3.7**
O4	87.9	−3.5***	−0.5	2.5	−0.4
O5	81.4	−10.9***	−5.7**	−9.6	−8.8*

NOTE: *** = statistically significant from zero at the 1 percent level; ** = statistically significant from zero at the 5 percent level; * = statistically significant from zero at the 10 percent level.

For black men, we find slightly lower promotion in the early career, and no difference in retention up to promotion to O3. While the difference in retention as an O1 is statistically significant, the magnitude is only one-tenth of a percentage point. We find larger differences in promotion and retention beginning with the O3 retention window. The percentage of black male officers who are retained as an O3 is 4.8 points higher than white male officers, while the percentage that are promoted to O4 is 2.6 points lower. Given promotion to O4, however, retention as an O4 is 1.7 points higher for black men. Similarly, black male officers are less likely to be promoted to O5 (4.3 percentage points lower) but more likely stay given promotion, by 2.5 percentage points. They are also less likely to be promoted to O6, though the O6 promotion effect for this group is not precisely estimated and is not statistically different from zero.

The results for black male officers are consistent with the findings of the earlier RAND study. The earlier study also found that black men were less likely to be promoted, but were more likely to be retained, given promotion. The magnitudes of the effects are also about the same.

The results for Hispanic men are quite similar to the ones for black men. As in the case of blacks, we find larger effects in the field grades of O4 through O6 and find that Hispanics are less likely to be promoted but more likely to stay given promotion, relative to white men. One difference relative to black males is that Hispanic males are even less likely to be promoted to O6. Specifically, we find that relative to white males, Hispanic males are 7.7 percentage points less likely to be promoted to O6, given retention as an O5.

Finally, the results for other minority male officers are quite similar to those for the other minority groups. The other group includes Asians, Pacific islanders, Alaskan natives, American Indians, those who are designated as "other race," and those for whom race is unknown.

Table 3.2 shows the estimated differences for female officers. The results for white and minority women differ from those of minority men, and the results differ across the female officer groups, unlike the case with minority male officers, for whom the results were fairly similar. It is useful to consider the results for the early career and later career separately. While we find statistically significant differences from white men in the likelihood of women reaching both early and later career milestones, in general the differences are larger in the later career, though not always statistically significant. Also, generally speaking, we find that both white and minority women are less likely to be promoted and are generally less likely to stay given promotion up to and including the O5 milestone. However, we find that female officers are generally more likely to be promoted to O6 given eligibility. Finally, we find that the results for black female officers often differ from those of the other female officer groups we consider. Black women generally stay at about the same rate as white men, though they are more likely to stay at the O3 milestone and likely to stay after promotion to O5. Also, unlike other female officers, eligible black female officers are less likely to be promoted to O6.

More specifically, in the early career, female officers are less likely to be promoted to O2, O3, and O4 than white males are, with the exception that black women are about as likely to be promoted to O3 as white men are. We also find that, with the exception of black women, retention rates for female officers at O3 are also generally lower than those for white males. White female officers at O3 have a notably low retention rate: The percentage of white female O3 officers who stay until eligibility for promotion to O4 is 10.9 points less than it is for white males. For Hispanic women, the rate is 4.7 percentage points lower and for other minority women, the rate is 3.7 points lower.

The early career results differ for black women. We find that the likelihood of promotion to O3 for this group is not statistically different from the likelihood for white male officers, given they stayed to be eligible for an O3 promotion. Furthermore, the percentage of black females who stay as an O3, given promotion to O3, is 4.2 points higher than it is for white males. This result suggests that black female officers have similar promotion rates as white male officers to O3 and higher retention as an O3, unlike white, Hispanic, and other minority female officers, who have lower promotion and lower retention at these milestones.

The results for female officers in the early career are consistent with the earlier RAND study. Like that study, we find that white women are less likely to stay during retention periods and somewhat less likely than white men to be promoted. Also, like the earlier study, we find differences in both retention and promotion for black female officers. We also find, like the earlier study, higher retention at the O3 point for black women.

Focusing now on the later career milestones through O5, we find that the differences in the likelihood of achieving later career milestones are more dramatic for both white and minority women. In the case of white female officers, the larger differences compared with white males in the later career are in retention rather than promotion. In contrast, the larger differences in the later career for black female officers generally occur in promotion rather retention. For example, white women are slightly more likely to be promoted to O5 (by 0.6 percentage points, and the effect is not precisely estimated), while black female officers are much less likely to be promoted to both O4 (3.9 percentage points) and O5 (6.8 percentage points). Both white and black female officers are less likely to stay as an O5 than their white male counterparts, but the differences are larger for white women (10.9 points as an O5 versus 5.7 for black women).

The later promotion patterns through O5 for Hispanic female officers appear to resemble those for their black female counterparts, though the promotion effects in the later career are not statistically significant for Hispanics, perhaps owing to small sample sizes. Hispanic female officers are less likely to be promoted to O4 and to O5, with point estimates that are similar to those of black female officers but that are not precisely estimated, mostly due to small sample sizes. Like white and black female officers, Hispanic female officers are less likely to stay as an O5, given promotion to that point. While the effect is relatively large, at –9.6 percentage points, it is not statistically significant.

The later promotion patterns through O5 for other minority female officers resemble those for their white female counterparts. Like white female officers, other minority female officers are less likely to be promoted to O4. We find no statistical difference at the O5 promotion, perhaps owing to the small sample size. While white female officers are substantially less likely to stay as an O3, this effect is smaller (3.7 percentage points) for other minority female officers. Like the other female officer groups, those in the other minority category are much less likely to stay as an O5. The percentage of other minority female officers that stay as an O5 is 8.8 percentage points lower than the percentage for white males.

As mentioned, female officers are more likely than white male officers to be promoted to O6, given retention to that career point, except for black women. The difference is especially large for other minority female officers, who we find are 16.6 percentage points more likely to be promoted to O6 than white male officers, given retention. The difference is also large for Hispanic females, at 13.1 points, though not statistically significant, and is more modest but still statistically significant for white female officers, at 3.4 points. In contrast, given retention as an O5, black female officers are less likely than white males to be promoted to O6, by 7.7 percentage points, and the difference is statistically significant.

The earlier study had small samples of black and other minority women and so was unable to detect differences at later career stages. This is also a problem in this study for the analysis of Hispanic women. We do find that black women continue to be less likely than white men to be promoted at the later career stages of O5 and O6, and the results are statistically significant. In contrast to the O3 point, we find that black women are less likely to stay as an O5 and that they are less likely to be promoted to that point.

Likelihood of Achieving Early and Later Career Milestones

The results in Tables 3.1 and 3.2 focus on each career milestone, conditional on achieving the previous one, and allow us to separately focus on the retention and promotion results. We next consider results regarding the likelihood an entering officer would achieve a promotion to O4 and the likelihood that an officer who reached O4 is ultimately promoted to O6. This analysis allows us to ascertain the net or joint effects of retention and promotion differences. Table 3.3 shows the results for male and female officers, with regression results shown in the appendix.

We find that, on net, male entrants who are white or Hispanic have nearly identical likelihoods of reaching O4, while black and other minority men have higher likelihoods of reaching O4. However, the results in Table 3.2 illustrate that the paths to O4 differ for black and Hispanic men compared with white men. Black and Hispanic men are less likely to be promoted through O4 but are more likely to stay, given promotion. For Hispanic men, these effects are completely offsetting, so Hispanic entrants have virtually the same likelihood of promotion to O4 as their white counterparts. For black men, the retention effect more than offsets the promotion effect, so black men are more likely to reach O4 than white men are. This result contrasts with the earlier RAND study, which found that the retention and promotion effects

Table 3.3
Likelihood of an Entry Cohort Reaching Promotion and Retention Milestones

	Percentage of Entering Officer Cohort Reaching:	
	O1 to O4 Promotion	O4 to O6 Promotion
Male officers		
White	45.4	23.6
Black	47.2***	19.5***
Hispanic	45.9	20.1
Other	48.4***	21.0
Female officers		
White	30.8***	18.8***
Black	45.3	15.6***
Hispanic	36.4***	23.1
Other	37.2***	26.8

NOTE: *** = statistically significant from zero at the 1 percent level; ** = statistically significant from zero at the 5 percent level; * = statistically significant from zero at the 10 percent level.

were completely offsetting for black men. As seen in Table 3.1, promotion rates through O4 for other minority men are similar to those for white men, but other minority men are more likely to stay given promotion to O3. The net effect is positive, and so men from this group are more likely to achieve O4 than white men.

We find that black, Hispanic, and other minority men who reached O4 are less likely than their white counterparts to ultimately achieve O6, though only the difference for black men is estimated with precision. White men are estimated to have a 23.6 percent likelihood of achieving O6, given they reached O4, while 19.5 percent of black men and Hispanic men reach O6. As seen in Table 3.1, although black men are more likely to stay given promotion, they are less likely to be promoted to O5 and O6 than white men. The negative promotion effects more than offset the positive retention effects, so the net effect is a lower likelihood of reaching O6, given achievement of O4.

Turning next to female officers, we find that, on net, female entrants are less likely to achieve O4 than their male counterparts, with the exception of black women, for whom the difference is not statistically significant. Among female officers, white women are the least likely to achieve O4 (30.8 percent), while black women are the most likely (45.3 percent), but both groups are less likely than their male counterparts (45.2 percent for white men and 47.2 for black men). As shown in Table 3.1, the lower likelihood of reaching O4 is in part due to lower promotion and in part due to lower retention through O4. The relative importance of retention and promotion varies with group. For white women, the biggest factor is their lower likelihood of staying as an O3, added to the effect of somewhat lower promotion through O4. For black women, the dominating factor is lower promotion to O4 despite higher retention as an O3. For Hispanic women and other minority women, both lower promotion to O2 and O3 and lower retention as an O3 are contributing factors.

We find that, on net, white, Hispanic, and black female officers are less likely to achieve O6, given they reached O4, though the results for Hispanic women are more uncertain given the lack of precise point estimates for promotion in the later career. Black women are especially less likely to achieve O6 than white or black men (15.8 percent compared with 23.6 percent and 19.5 percent, respectively). For the most part, the especially lower rate for black women reflects their lower likelihood of promotion to O5 and to O6, though it is also partially due to a lower likelihood of staying as an O5. Hispanic women are less likely to be promoted to O5 and less likely to stay given promotion to O5, though neither difference is statistically significantly different from zero, perhaps due to small sample sizes. Hispanic women are more likely to be promoted to O6 (again not statistically significant). The higher O6 promotion rate offsets the lower O5 promotion and retention rates to some degree. The pattern for white women is broadly similar to the one for Hispanic women, though the effects are generally statistically significant.

Finally, we find that other minority women are more likely to reach O6, conditional on achieving O4, than any other group we examined, including white males, though the difference is not statistically different from zero. In large part, this result is driven by the higher estimated likelihood of promotion to O6 for other minority women; we find that this group is 16.6 percentage points more likely to achieve O6 promotion, given retention in the O5 window.

CHAPTER FOUR

Results on Female Officer Career Progression Differences in Restricted Occupations

In this chapter, we present our results on differences in the career progression of female officers in occupations partially closed to women, relative to those in open occupations. As we discuss in Chapter Two, our approach involves estimating these differences net of the differences for men. We also control for other factors, as before, including source of commission, service, cumulative deployment, education, broad occupational area, and prior enlisted service. We use the differences in career progression of men in these partially closed occupations relative to occupations that are open as a control for how career progression differs in general in these restricted occupations. Again, we remind the reader that our approach allows us to describe differences in career progression for women in partially closed occupations, but, because we do not control for all factors that affect career progression differences and the potential problems of using men as a control group, we cannot interpret our findings as estimates of the effects that partial closure has on career progression of female officers.

Table 4.1 summarizes the key results of the analysis. The figures in the second and third columns show the percentage of male officers and female officers, respectively, reaching each milestone who are in occupations that are open. The percentages are conditional on reaching the previous milestone. The percentages for men are comparable to the overall conditional percentages shown in Table 2.2 in Chapter Two, while the differences in the percentages between women and men are comparable to the estimated differences for women shown in Table 3.2 in Chapter Three.

The fourth and fifth columns in Table 4.1 show the estimated difference between (1) the percentage of officers reaching each career milestone for those in partially closed occupations and (2) the same percentage in open occupations for men and for women, respectively. The differences for women show how career progression differs for women in occupations partially closed to women relative to open ones.[1] We find no statistical difference in likelihood of promotion to O4, O5, and O6 among women in partially closed occupations, but we observe that retention as an O3 and O5 is lower in these occupations.

These observed differences for women could be due to differences in the nature of the occupations, and career progression may differ across occupations partially closed to women relative to open ones, regardless of gender. As mentioned, we use the difference for men as our

---

[1] The second and third columns of Table 4.1 are means, conditional on being in an open occupation. The fourth and sixth columns of Table 4.1 are parameter estimates from our regression models, reported in Table A.7 in the appendix. The fifth column is a linear combination of the fourth and sixth column, and we test for statistical significance of the linear combination.

Table 4.1
Estimated Percentage Point Differences in the Likelihood of Reaching Promotion and Retention Milestones for Women in Partially Closed Occupations

	Percentage of Male Officers Retained or Promoted in Open Occupations	Percentage of Female Officers Retained or Promoted in Open Occupations	Percentage Point Difference for Men: Partially Closed – Open Occupations for Male Officers	Percentage Point Difference for Women: Partially Closed – Open Occupations for Female Officers	Difference for Female Versus Male Officers: Percentage Point Difference for Women – Percentage Point Difference for Men
Promotion:					
O3 to O4	74.5	69.9	4.6***	1.4	-3.2**
O4 to O5	73.5	73.0	0.8	1.3	0.5
O5 to O6	46.3	47.3	3.1*	-1.6	-4.7
Retention as:					
O3	72.7	60.8	-8.4***	-2.2**	6.2***
O4	88.0	87.5	1.9***	0.2	-1.6
O5	81.6	69.2	-5.2***	-6.5*	-1.3

NOTE: *** = statistically significant difference at the 1 percent level; ** = statistically significant difference at the 5 percent level; * = statistically significant difference at the 10 percent level.

control comparison, showing how career progression generally differs in the partially closed occupations relative to the open ones. The results for men suggest that male officers experience a higher likelihood of promotion to O4, O5, and O6 in occupations partially closed to women, though the difference is not statistically significant for O5. The results also indicate that men in the partially closed occupations are less likely to stay after promotion to O3 and after promotion to O5.

The key results of interest are in the final column of Table 4.1, which shows the differences in career progression for women in partially closed occupations relative to those in open occupations, net of the difference for men. That is, the final column of the table shows the difference between (1) the percentage point difference for women in partially closed versus open occupations (fifth column of Table 4.1) and (2) the percentage point difference for men in partially closed versus open occupations (fourth column of Table 4.1). The results suggest some differences in retention as an O3 and promotion to O4 but no statistically significant differences beyond that. Specifically, we find evidence to suggest that women in restricted occupations are more likely to stay after being promoted to O3, by 6.2 percentage points. While our point estimates indicate that they are also less likely to stay after being promoted to O4 and to O5, neither of these differences is statistically significantly different from zero.

The promotion results are not clear-cut. Women who are in partially closed occupations are less likely to be promoted to O4 by 3.2 percentage points, given they reach eligibility, and less likely to be promoted to O6. However, only the O4 difference is statistically significant.

One approach to better understanding the implications of the results in Table 4.1 is to consider the net effect of the promotion and retention results, given an officer reached O4. The results are reported in Table 4.2.

We estimate that 22.9 percent of male officers at O4 who are not in an occupation partially closed to women will achieve an O6 promotion. The estimate reflects the joint effect of the likelihood of reaching each career milestone shown in the second column of Table 4.1. In contrast, the percentage of O4 male officers reaching O6 in partially closed occupations is 24.6. The net effect for male officers is 1.7 percentage points, a difference that is not statistically significant. That is, on net, for a male officer who has reached O4, there is no statistically significant difference between his likelihood of achieving O6 if he is in a partially closed occupation vesus an open one.

We find that female officers in open occupations are less likely to reach O6, given promotion to O4, than men. This is consistent with the findings in Table 3.3 in Chapter Three, where we found that female officers in general were less likely than men to reach O4.

Table 4.2
Percentage of Officers Reaching O6 in Open Versus Partially Closed Occupations, Conditional on Reaching O4

	Male Officers	Female Officers	Difference for Female Versus Male Officers
Open	22.9	18.9***	
Partially closed	24.6	19.2	
Net effect	1.7	0.3	−1.4

NOTE: *** = statistically significant from male officers at the 1 percent level; ** = statistically significant from male officers at the 5 percent level; * = statistically significant from male officers at the 10 percent level.

Table 4.2 also shows the estimated difference in the likelihood of female officers reaching O6 in open versus closed occupations. The net difference is less than 1 percentage point, 0.3 points, and is not statistically different from zero. Thus, on net, there is no difference in likelihood of reaching O6 for women in partially closed versus open occupations, given they reached O6.

The lack of an estimated difference for women might be attributable to differences in promotion and retention in open versus partially closed occupations, and we need to control for these differences. We do this by subtracting out the difference for men. This is shown in the far right column in Table 4.2. The 0.3 percentage point difference for women minus the 1.7 percentage point difference for men yields a difference for women of −1.4 percentage points, a difference that is not statistically significant from zero. Thus, we estimate that female officers in partially closed occupations have the same likelihood of achieving O6, conditional on having achieved O4, as women in open occupations, relative to men.

The results of this analysis suggest that, on net, women in restricted occupations do no worse and no better than women in unrestricted occupations, compared with the experience of men in these occupations. These results by no means imply that lifting restrictions on service by women in these partially closed occupations will have no effect on their prospects of reaching O6. The results cannot be interpreted as causal. More generally, this analysis does not shed light on how lifting restrictions on service by women would affect their career progression. It does shed light on how cohorts of female officers have fared in occupations that are partially closed relative to those who are in ones that are open, net of the differences for men, and controlling for other factors. In sum, we find that female officers in these partially closed occupations who have achieved O4 have not fared worse or better in terms of their progression to O6.

Summary and Conclusions

Given that our analysis is an update of an earlier study, the natural question is to what degree do we observe improvements or degradation in the career progression of minorities and women compared with what was found in the earlier study? In the previous chapter, we noted that many of our results are consistent with those of the earlier study in terms of the direction of effects. However, the magnitude of the effects differ, so it is possible that we can observe improvement or lack of improvement for some groups. The first part of this chapter summarizes our findings and draws conclusions regarding our updated analysis of minority and gender differences in career progression. It then considers the key findings and conclusions from our analysis of differences in female officer career progression in partially closed occupations versus all occupations. It concludes with a discussion of unanswered questions and areas for possible further work.

Comparison of Results with Those of the Earlier RAND Study

We note that any comparison of our results with those og the earlier study must be considered rather exploratory, for several reasons. Our data are monthly data (except in the early years when they are quarterly), while the earlier study had access only to annual data. Because accession of female officers increased, especially minority female officers, we have larger sample sizes for these groups in the updated study. The earlier study focused its conclusions largely on the earlier part of the officer career, through promotion to O4, though sample size issues did not prevent analysis of later career progression differences for black men. Since the data sets are different, we cannot test for statistical significance between our results and the earlier results. Also, we use additional control variables, such as deployment experience, a variable that was not relevant for the earlier study. Finally, the results for minorities were largely limited to black officers in the previous study and to differences in the early career, whereas we are able to further investigate differences later in the career and to consider differences for Hispanic officers and other minorities as well, though we again acknowledge that the analysis here also suffers from small sample sizes for Hispanic women.

The top of Table 5.1 replicates the earlier study findings regarding the net or joint effect of promotion and retention in the early career, through O4. That is, it shows the estimated percentage of entering officers reaching O4, accounting for differences in promotion and retention, by race and gender. For comparison's sake, we show the corresponding results from this study for these same groups. These results are also shown in Table 3.3 in Chapter Three. We also include our results for the other race/ethnicity groups we consider, as well as our results for

Table 5.1
Percentage of Entering Officers Reaching Promotion and Retention Milestones: Earlier RAND Study and Updated Study Results

	O1 Through O4 Promotion		O4 Through O6 Promotion	
	Percentage	Difference from White Men	Percentage	Difference from White Men
Hosek et al. (2001)				
White men	37			
Black men	36	–1		
White women	30	–7		
Black women	31	–6		
Updated study				
White men	45.4		23.6	
Black men	47.2	1.8***	19.5	–4.1***
Hispanic men	45.9	0.4	20.1	–3.5
Other minority men	48.4	3.0***	21.0	–2.6
White women	30.8	–14.6***	18.8	–4.8***
Black women	45.3	–0.1	15.6	–8.0***
Hispanic women	36.4	–9.0***	23.1	–0.5
Other minority women	37.2	–8.2***	26.8	3.2

NOTE: *** = statistically significant from white male officers at the 1 percent level;
** = statistically significant from white male officers at the 5 percent level;
* = statistically significant from white male officers at the 10 percent level.

the later career (O4 through O6). Again, these results are from Table 3.3. As we discussed in the context of Table 2.2 in Chapter Two, retention increased between this study and the earlier one, and promotion changed a bit as well. Thus, not surprisingly, Table 5.1 shows that the likelihood of reaching O4 is higher in our study, regardless of race or gender.

Consider first a comparison of the results of the earlier study with the current one for the groups in common, specifically white and black men and women in grades O1 through O4 promotion. Our results for black men relative to white men are a bit different from the findings from the earlier study. Like the earlier study, we find that black men are less likely to be promoted up to and including O4, but more likely to stay given promotion. In the earlier study, the net effect is that the likelihood for black men of reaching O4 is the same as for white men, whereas in our study, the retention effect offsets the promotion effect and black men are more likely to reach O4. This is seen in Table 5.1, where we find an increased likelihood of reaching O4.

For white women, we find that, compared with white men, the likelihood of reaching O4 was 7 percentage points lower in the earlier study but is 14.6 percentage points lower in the updated study. The results for black women are in some ways just the opposite. The earlier study found that, relative to white men, black women entrants were 6 percentage points less likely to reach the O4 point in their career, while the updated study finds no statistically significant difference.

Recall from Table 2.1 in Chapter Two that we use information on officer cohorts entering between 1986 and 2002 to analyze promotion through O3 and information from cohorts as early as 1983 to analyze promotion through O4. The earlier study used information from officer cohorts entering as early as 1967 and as late as 1991 to analyze promotion and retention through O4. Thus, there is some overlap in the cohorts analyzed between the two studies. While we do not know whether the differences we observe between the studies are statistically significant, the larger difference in the updated analysis for white women suggests that the likelihood of reaching O4 does not appear to be higher for white women among more recent cohorts, and may well be lower. Similarly, the smaller difference in the updated study for black women suggests that the likelihood of reaching O4 appears higher, or at least no lower, than it was in the earlier study.

The earlier study was not able to examine Hispanic and other minority women, due to limited sample size. Thus, we are unable to compare our results with earlier results. Our results for these groups also suffer from small sample size to some degree, but the results in Table 5.1 are suggestive. We find that Hispanic men have the same likelihood of reaching O4 as white men. On the other hand, other minority men are more likely to reach O4. The results in the early career for Hispanic and other minority female officers are broadly similar to those for white women; relative to white men, women in these groups are less likely to reach O4.

In sum, the updated result for black men on the likelihood of reaching O4 differs somewhat from that found in the earlier study, though our results on career progression are similar. Like that study, we find that black men are less likely to be promoted but more likely to stay given promotion; however, the effects are offsetting in the early study but not in this study. We find consistent results with the earlier study for both white and black female officers, though the magnitude of effects differ somewhat. In the updated analysis, we find that, compared with white men, the gap in the likelihood of reaching O4 is larger for white women, but smaller (and actually not statistically different) for black women. The changes in results for women are due primarily to changes in retention, with white women and black women diverging further in the updated study. On net, our results suggest, relative to the earlier study, an increased likelihood of achieving O4 for black men, an improvement as well for black women, and a worsening for white women. While we are not able to make comparisons with the earlier study for Hispanic and other minority officers, we find that Hispanic men have similar results as white men, while other minority men are more likely to reach O4 than white men. The results through O4 for Hispanic and other minority women are quite similar to those for white women in our study.

New Results for the Later Career

The updated study allows us to consider the likelihood of reaching later career milestones, from O4 to O6 (the right-most two columns in Table 4.1 in Chapter Four). For black men, we find a higher likelihood of reaching O4 but a negative difference in the later career; the lower likelihood of being promoted to O5 for black men is only partially offset by their higher likelihood of staying, given promotion to O5. The results for Hispanic men and for other minority men are similar to that of black men, except that the differences are not statistically significant.

For white female officers in the later career, we find that the gap is smaller than it was in the early career (4.8 percentage points rather than 14.6). Thus, the updated study suggests that while the likelihood of achieving O4 is no better (and may be worse) than in the earlier study, white women appear to gain some ground in the later career, relative to white men, though they do not completely close the gap in the likelihood of achieving O6. We find that in the later career, the gap for black women seems to widen, relative to earlier in the career. Relative to white men, black women are substantially less likely to reach O6, given they reached O4, compared with no gap in the early career. These results suggest that achievement of the early career milestone of O4 has improved for black women, or at least not worsened, relative to the earlier study. However, the progress in the early career is not sustained in the later career for black women, relative to white men. In interpreting these findings, it is important to note that the results for the later career are based on earlier (older) cohorts, while results for the early career are based on later (younger cohorts). Thus, our results may be due to differences in behavior across different entering cohorts and not actual differences in career progression at different stages of the career.

Similar to what we find for white women, we find a larger gap relative to white males in the early career and a smaller gap in the later career for both Hispanic and other minority women, though neither difference in the later career is statistically significant. The point estimate for other minority women is actually positive, indicating a higher likelihood of achieving O6 than their white male counterparts, though again the difference is not precisely estimated.

Thus, our results suggest that the higher likelihood for black than white men of achieving the earlier career milestone of O4 slips in the later career, so that black men are less likely to achieve O6, given they reached O4. We find similar results for black women; they have the same likelihood as white men of achieving O4 but a lower likelihood of achieving O6. Thus, the narrowing of the gap in the early career for black women, compared with that found in the earlier study, does not appear to be sustained in the later career. On the other hand, the results for white women suggest a narrowing of differences in the later career. In large part, the narrowing is due to a higher likelihood of promotion to O6, given retention to the O6 promotion window.

In sum, our analysis indicates that female officer career progression differences relative to white male officers are attributable to both retention and to promotion, with the importance of each varying depending on the group. Our analysis indicates that, on net, minority men are as likely or, in the case of black and other minority men, more likely to reach the O4 milestone than white men. However, we find that black men are less likely to achieve O6 than white men because of differences in career progression in the field grades of O4 through O6.

Career Progression in Occupations Partially Closed to Women

Our study also investigates how career progression for female officers in occupations partially closed to women compares to progression in open occupations. We find that, on net, relative to men, women in partially closed occupations are as likely as women in open occupations to reach O6, given they had reached O4.

These results are somewhat surprising. Our expectation was that restrictions would limit the career progression of women, and so we expected that women in partially closed occupations would fare worse than women in open occupations. However, we find no statistically significant difference. We have several possible conjectures about why we find this result. One explanation is that our analysis is conditioned on an officer achieving O4. It is possible that differences in career progression for women in partially closed occupations occur early in the career. We have some evidence of such differences: Table 4.1 in the previous chapter shows that women in partially closed occupations are less likely to be promoted than women in open occupations. Thus, these women may fare worse early on, but, conditional on making it to O4, they fare about the same. Another possible explanation is that we do not control for all of the qualifications and performance metrics of officers in our analysis, though we do control for education, prior enlisted service, and source of commission. Female officers in partially closed occupations may be better qualified, more motivated, or possibly perform better, leading to a higher chance of reaching O6 and offsetting any negative effect of restrictions. A related explanation is that women in partially closed occupations may perceive that their ability to be promoted is hampered by the restrictions on women's service and so they take additional actions, pursue additional training and education opportunities, and find other ways to offset the disadvantage. The net effect, observed in the data, is that their likelihood of achieving O6, given they achieved O4, is not adversely affected. A final explanation is that the restrictions are not binding; there may be insufficient numbers of women who enter partially closed occupations for the closures to severely restrict career opportunities.

To better understand the results, more information is therefore needed about the specific occupations, the assignment patterns of female and male officers, the qualifications and performance of officers in these occupations, and the criteria used for promotion. Again, we reiterate that our findings do not indicate the causal effect that partially closing occupations has on the career progression of women, nor the effect that lifting restrictions has on the service of female members. Furthermore, the focus of the analysis is on occupations partially closed to women. We have no information on how the career progression of women would fare if occupations that are fully closed were opened.

Unanswered Questions

This report describes differences in officer career progression by minority and gender status and by whether occupations are partially closed. The analysis of minority and gender status updates the earlier RAND study. Still, there are a number of questions that it does not address.

First, the analysis does not indicate whether recent entry officer cohorts will experience the same career progression as described here. The reason is that our data on career progression, especially in the more senior grades, are drawn from older entry cohorts, as shown in Table 2.1 in Chapter Two. Whether recent entrants will have the same experiences as past entrants is unclear.

Second, while our data cover a period when some of the restrictions on women's service were lifted or redefined, especially in the 1992–1994 period, our analysis does not indicate how lifting those restrictions affected the career progression of female officers. Answering this question is hampered by the lack of data on the "counterfactual." That is, we do not know what the career progression of women would have been in occupations that were closed, because there are no data on women in these occupations during the period when the occupations were closed. Thus, we can consider the career progression only of women in partially closed occupations, and these occupations may differ in important ways, in terms of career progression, from fully closed ones.

Assessing the effects of lifting restrictions on women's career progression requires information on women's behavioral response to the lifting of restrictions, such as changes in their occupational choices and in their retention decisions. One approach to obtaining this information is to estimate a structural model of the occupational decisions and retention decisions of female officers over their career and conduct simulations of how lifting restrictions would affect these decisions. Such an approach has been used to study the behavioral responses of officers and enlisted personnel to changes in compensation and to up-or-out rules (Mattock, Hosek, and Asch, forthcoming; Asch and Warner, 2001). Such an analysis would require longitudinal data on the occupational choices and retention choices of female officers and model estimates of the underlying parameters that guide these decisions. An intermediate step would be to model career progression, especially in occupational areas and assignments closed to women, and simulate the effects on career progression of alternative policies that lift restrictions on service by women, without accounting for the behavioral response. An intermediate model would require information on assignment patterns in these occupations, as well as information on promotion and retention of women and men, and specifically the information provided in this report. The intermediate model could then estimate how lifting restrictions on the service of women would affect promotion opportunities in general and for women specifically.

Third, our analysis includes variables that control for other factors that could explain differences in career progression, such as source of commission. Nonetheless, these are imperfect and do not control for a myriad of other factors that might explain differences in career progression, especially by gender and minority status. These might include differences in entry characteristics, including ability and proficiencies; differences in performance and opportunities, such as opportunities for command experience and access to mentors and peer networks; and the occupational choices (at a more micro level than we consider) made by officers. Insofar as these factors vary with gender or minority group, they could explain some of the differences in career progression that we find in this study.

Detailed Description of Data and Methods, and Regression Results

This appendix offers greater detail than we provided in Chapter Two on the data we use and how we define key variables in the analysis. It also presents our regression results.

Officer Cohort Files and Variable Definitions

As discussed in Chapter Two, the longitudinal data set used in the statistical analysis in this report was created using DMDC's Proxy-PERSTEMPO file. The file contains longitudinal administrative records on active-duty personnel by month from January 1993 through September 2010 and for the last month in each quarter going back to October 1987. The data include a snapshot of every member on active duty in a given month or quarter and track members until they separate from active duty or until the end of the file in 2010.

We use these data to create a longitudinal database that follows the 1971–2002 officer cohorts as they progress through various stages of their careers, shown in Table 2.1 in Chapter Two.

Our analysis contains two types of control variables: (1) those, such as race, gender, and source of commission, that are static over time and (2) those, such as months of deployment and the officer's military occupatonal specialty (MOS), that may change over time. We measured static control variables at the time of entry into the Proxy-PERSTEMPO database. Thus, for cohorts entering prior to 1988, this occurs in the fourth quarter of 1987, the first year of data in the Proxy-PERSTEMPO database. For cohorts entering during or after 1988, this occurs in the month of entry.

We also include a static variable indicating whether the officer had prior service upon entry as an officer. We use the officer's base entry service date (BASD) to infer prior service. For officers entering prior to 1988, we compare their BASD to the their date of commission; if the BASD indicates entry into the service as one or more years prior to the date of commission, we code the officer as having prior service. For officers entering in 1988 or later, we compare their BASD with the date at which they enter the Proxy-PERSTEMPO database as an O1; if an officer's BASD indicates entry into the service as one or more years prior to entry as an O1, we code the officer as having prior service.

For models of retention at O1 and promotion to O2, we measured dynamic control variables at the time of entry. For models of retention and promotion at higher ranks, we measured dynamic control variables at the time of the most recent promotion. Thus, for example, in models of retention at O5, dynamic control variables are measured during the month or quarter when the officer was promoted to O5, while, in models of promotion to O3, dynamic control variables are measured at the O2 promotion point. Dynamic control variables in our analysis include marital status, education, two-digit DoD occupation codes,[1] and cumulative months of deployment since the previous promotion point.

We created the promotion and retention variables according to schedules of promotion for each cohort and service that we observed in the data. We define retention at O1 as persisting until the onset of the promotion window to O2. Conditional upon being retained at O1, we define promotion to O2 as progressing to O2 within the O2 promotion window. Conditional on having been promoted to Oi, we define retention at Oi as persisting until the onset of the Oi+1 promotion window. Conditional upon being retained at Oj, we define promotion to Oj+1 as progressing to Oj+1 within the Oj+1 promotion window.

We do not have data that explicitly define the promotion windows for each cohort and service. We thus followed Hosek et al. (2001) by imputing promotion windows based on the observed distribution of time to promotion for each cohort and service. In particular, for each cell defined by quarter-of-entry cohort and service, we track all service members from time of entry in our database until promotion to O6 or 2010, the last year of our data. To define the window for promotion to Oi, we find the total number of promotions to Oi occurring during each possible six-month window from 1988 until 2010 and choose the six-month window where we observe the most promotions. We define this six-month window plus the 15 months prior and 15 months after as the three-year Oi promotion window. We require that the imputed promotion window capture at least 80 percent of all promotions for the relevant service/cohort cell, and we require all imputed windows to start and end within the 22-year period spanned by our data. If the imputed Oi promotion window does not meet these criteria, we do not include officers from the associated service and cohort in analyses of retention at Oi-1 or promotion to Oi. Following this strategy, we are able to impute promotion windows that capture over 95 percent of all promotions to each rank from O2 to O6.

Our strategy for imputing promotion windows requires us to assign each officer an entry quarter. We assign officers entering as an O1 in 1988 or later to the quarter in which they entered the officer ranks as an O1. For service members entering prior to 1988, we do not observe entry as an O1. We thus match service members to an entry cohort based on the date of their first observed promotion. We group all officers from pre-1988 entry cohorts into cells defined by service and the rank and quarter of their first observed promotion. Thus, for officers entering our database as O3s in 1988, we restrict attention to those who were promoted to O4, group those officers into cells defined by service and quarter of promotion to O4, and analyze the following outcomes: retention at O4, promotion to O5, retention at O5, and promotion to O6.

Control Variables by Race/Ethnicity and Gender

We explored how the control variables differ by race/ethnicity and gender. Since we use cohorts through 2002, we consider differences in entry cohorts only through 2002.

---

[1]   Note that we treat DoD occupation codes differently than Hosek et al. (2001). In particular, Hosek et al. used one-digit DoD occupation codes during the fourth year of service (or at exit for officers who separate before the fourth year). Hosek et al. note that there is little change in one-digit occupation codes after the fourth year of service. In contrast, there is significant movement across occupations at the two-digit level. Hence, we use the two-digit DoD occupation code at the previous promotion point.

Table A.1
Percentage of Officer Accessions in Each Service for Selected Years by Race, Ethnicity, and Gender (excluding profession occupations)

	White Male	Black Male	Hispanic Male	Other Male	White Female	Black Female	Hispanic Female	Other Female
1988								
Army	74.3	9.7	2.3	3.9	5.6	3.0	0.3	1.0
Navy	82.4	3.7	3.2	3.3	6.2	0.6	0.2	0.3
Marine Corps	84.7	4.5	3.5	4.5	2.0	0.3	0.0	0.5
Air Force	78.9	4.0	1.1	5.0	8.6	1.3	0.2	0.9
DoD total	79.6	5.3	2.3	4.1	6.4	1.4	0.2	0.7
1996								
Army	69.7	7.6	4.1	5.8	8.3	2.8	0.8	0.9
Navy	72.6	5.9	5.0	6.3	7.6	1.1	0.6	0.9
Marine Corps	74.8	7.9	4.7	4.9	6.1	0.8	0.4	0.6
Air Force	71.4	4.7	1.9	7.3	11.8	1.5	0.3	1.2
DoD total	71.6	6.4	3.8	6.2	8.8	1.7	0.6	0.9
2002								
Army	59.3	9.4	5.0	8.0	10.3	4.2	1.4	2.4
Navy	70.2	5.9	5.6	5.6	9.6	1.1	0.7	1.3
Marine Corps	74.2	5.1	6.2	5.9	6.2	0.9	0.9	0.6
Air Force	61.6	4.5	3.0	9.7	14.3	2.7	1.1	3.1
DoD total	64.0	6.5	4.6	7.8	11.2	2.7	1.1	2.2

Table A.1 shows the race/ethnicity and gender distributions for selected entry accession cohorts. In general, the Army and Air Force tend to be more diverse in terms of the gender and minority status of officer entrants who are not in the professional occupations. Table A.2 shows the percentage distribution of entrants in each group and cohort across commissioning source. White men (outside of the professional occupations) are generally more likely to be academy graduates, while minority men and both white and minority female officers are more likely to come from an ROTC program. Table A.3 shows the percentage of entrants in each group that have prior service. The percentage rose over time with more recent cohorts, for all groups, but especially for minority women between 1988 and 1996. The percentage doubled for this group over this time period. In the 2002 cohort and within gender groups, minorities were more likely to have prior service than were white officers. Table A.4 shows the occupational distribution at entry, by race/ethnicity and gender. Men are more likely than women to be in the "other" occupation group, which includes combat arms—an area generally closed to women.

Table A.2
**Commissioning Source of Entering Officers, by Gender and Minority Status, Selected Years
(percentage of race/gender group excluding profession occupations)**

	White Male	Minority Male	White Female	Minority Female
1988 cohort				
Academy	22.6	17.6	19.0	11.7
ROTC	49.6	55.3	57.3	70.2
Officer Candidate School	16.1	15.1	17.5	12.9
Direct appointment	5.8	5.6	4.4	2.0
Other/unknown	6.0	6.4	1.8	3.2
1996 cohort				
Academy	25.0	19.0	24.4	12.8
ROTC	42.9	48.0	49.4	61.5
Officer Candidate School	23.2	22.6	20.8	21.6
Direct appointment	1.4	2.2	1.7	2.0
Other/unknown	7.6	8.3	3.7	2.0
2002 cohort				
Academy	22.0	17.9	20.6	12.1
ROTC	36.5	41.1	47.8	55.7
Officer Candidate School	32.7	32.5	25.0	27.7
Direct appointment	1.0	1.5	1.6	1.0
Other/unknown	7.8	7.0	5.0	3.5

Table A.3
**Percentage of Entering Officers Who Have Prior Enlisted Service, Selected Years (percentage of
minority/gender group, excluding professional occupations)**

	White Male	Minority Male	White Female	Minority Female
1988	19.6	21.5	13.9	12.1
1996	24.9	28.1	16.2	25.1
2002	25.1	31.7	18.3	26.6

Regression Results

Table A.5 shows the results of the estimated probit models on minority and gender differences in career progression, corresponding to the results in Chapter Three. Table A.6 shows the results for the effect of minority and gender differences in the likelihood of reaching O4 and of reaching O6, conditional on having reached O4. Table A.7 shows the results for differences in partially closed occupations, corresponding to the results shown in Chapter Four. Table A.8 shows the results for differences in the likelihood of reaching O4 and of reaching

Table A.4
Distribution of Military Occupations, Selected Years (percentage of minority/gender group, excluding professional occupations)

	White Male	Minority Male	White Female	Minority Female
1988 cohort				
Tactical operations	19.0	23.1	12.0	9.7
Intelligence	2.9	2.5	11.7	14.2
Engineering and maintenance	11.3	13.2	18.3	16.2
Administration	2.7	5.2	29.1	30.4
Supply and procurement	5.0	8.5	10.3	19.8
Other	59.0	47.4	18.5	9.7
1996 cohort				
Tactical operations	26.3	27.9	11.7	10.6
General officers and executives	0.0	0.1	0.0	0.3
Intelligence	4.2	4.6	11.4	7.1
Engineering and maintenance	13.1	13.0	18.0	18.8
Administration	4.4	6.7	15.4	15.3
Supply and procurement	6.5	7.0	11.2	23.8
Other	45.5	40.8	32.5	24.1
2002 cohort				
Tactical operations	28.5	29.7	11.6	8.6
General officers and executives	2.0	1.1	1.3	0.7
Intelligence	3.4	3.9	8.4	10.9
Engineering and maintenance	13.7	16.9	21.4	30.3
Administration	3.4	4.2	9.6	11.6
Supply and procurement	5.2	8.7	13.2	16.5
Other	43.9	35.5	34.6	21.5

O6, condition on having reached O4, for women in partially closed occupations. Each column in Tables A.5–A.8 is the result of a separate regression for each career milestone. The last row of the tables shows the sample size for each regression. The table shows the marginal effect of each variable, i.e., the change in the probability of the outcome variable associated with a dummy variable taking the value of 1 versus 0. In the case of cumulative deployment, which is measured as months of deployment, the marginal effect is the change in the probability associated with an additional cumulative month of deployment. The tables also indicate standard errors and statistical significance levels. The regression models also include fixed effects for each entry cohort, but we do not report those estimates. The tables in Chapter Three report the coefficient estimates for the race/ethnicity and gender variables, and Table 4.1 in Chapter Four reports the estimates for the variables on whether an occupation is partially closed and on whether the officer is a female in a partially closed occupation.

Table A.5
Probit Regression Estimates of Minority and Gender Career Progression

Variable	(1) Retention as O1	(2) Promotion to O2	(3) Retention as O2	(4) Promotion to O3	(5) Retention as O3	(6) Promotion to O4	(7) Retention as O4	(8) Promotion to O5	(9) Retention as O5	(10) Promotion to O6
Prior service	0.0007***	0.0017***	0.0003	0.0224***	0.0805***	0.0141***	−0.0897***	−0.1655***	−0.1508***	−0.0141
	(0.0001)	(0.0006)	(0.0005)	(0.0014)	(0.0034)	(0.0037)	(0.0041)	(0.0057)	(0.0075)	(0.0101)
Navy	−0.0007**	0.0078***	0.0035***	0.0248***	−0.0151***	−0.1231***	−0.0467***	−0.1086***	0.0686***	−0.0420***
	(0.0003)	(0.0007)	(0.0004)	(0.0015)	(0.0036)	(0.0045)	(0.0044)	(0.0066)	(0.0072)	(0.0116)
Marine Corps	−0.0010*	0.0082***	0.0045***	−0.0278***	0.0366***	−0.0758***	−0.0147***	−0.1116***	0.0286	−0.0164
	(0.0005)	(0.0006)	(0.0004)	(0.0025)	(0.0052)	(0.0067)	(0.0065)	(0.0122)	(0.0204)	(0.0327)
Air Force	−0.0016***	0.0101***	0.0067***	0.0678***	0.0910***	−0.0347***	−0.0225***	−0.1479***	−0.0132*	−0.1016***
	(0.0003)	(0.0005)	(0.0004)	(0.0012)	(0.0031)	(0.0038)	(0.0041)	(0.0065)	(0.0071)	(0.0110)
ROTC	−0.0005***	−0.0011*	−0.0009**	−0.0569***	0.0559***	0.0049	0.0099***	−0.0594***	−0.0224***	−0.0821***
	(0.0002)	(0.0006)	(0.0004)	(0.0017)	(0.0031)	(0.0036)	(0.0035)	(0.0056)	(0.0065)	(0.0086)
Officer Candidate School/Training	−0.0003	−0.0036***	−0.0006	−0.0762***	0.0703***	−0.0149***	−0.0155***	−0.1071***	−0.0891***	−0.0968***
	(0.0003)	(0.0010)	(0.0007)	(0.0030)	(0.0038)	(0.0045)	(0.0043)	(0.0069)	(0.0080)	(0.0100)
Direct appointment	−0.0098***	−0.0187***	−0.0014	−0.0320***	0.0826***	0.0134*	−0.0420***	−0.0854***	−0.0885***	−0.0956***
	(0.0034)	(0.0041)	(0.0017)	(0.0062)	(0.0068)	(0.0076)	(0.0073)	(0.0108)	(0.0126)	(0.0145)
Unknown or other source of commission	−0.0017**	−0.0140***	−0.0009	−0.0760***	0.1108***	0.0064	−0.0373***	−0.0764***	0.0265	−0.1453***
	(0.0008)	(0.0026)	(0.0013)	(0.0054)	(0.0064)	(0.0077)	(0.0112)	(0.0177)	(0.0255)	(0.0346)
Black male	−0.0008**	−0.0112***	−0.0002	−0.0121***	0.0485***	−0.0264***	0.0176***	−0.0435***	0.0250**	−0.0251
	(0.0004)	(0.0014)	(0.0007)	(0.0024)	(0.0051)	(0.0060)	(0.0050)	(0.0089)	(0.0102)	(0.0166)
Hispanic male	−0.0002	−0.0046***	−0.0008	−0.0045	0.0241***	−0.0185**	0.0186**	−0.0463***	0.0274	−0.0768***
	(0.0004)	(0.0015)	(0.0010)	(0.0031)	(0.0073)	(0.0085)	(0.0077)	(0.0144)	(0.0171)	(0.0264)

Table A.5—Continued

Variable	(1) Retention as O1	(2) Promotion to O2	(3) Retention as O2	(4) Promotion to O3	(5) Retention as O3	(6) Promotion to O4	(7) Retention as O4	(8) Promotion to O5	(9) Retention as O5	(10) Promotion to O6
Other minority male	0.0002	−0.0009	0.0003	0.0015	0.0538***	−0.0039	0.0448***	−0.0384***	0.0304**	−0.0412*
	(0.0002)	(0.0011)	(0.0007)	(0.0024)	(0.0054)	(0.0064)	(0.0049)	(0.0111)	(0.0143)	(0.0231)
White female	−0.0003	−0.0078***	−0.0036***	−0.0255***	−0.1087***	−0.0324***	−0.0347***	0.0056	−0.1093***	0.0339**
	(0.0002)	(0.0012)	(0.0008)	(0.0024)	(0.0051)	(0.0061)	(0.0063)	(0.0081)	(0.0118)	(0.0158)
Black female	−0.0007	−0.0148***	−0.0023	−0.0021	0.0418***	−0.0388***	0.0052	−0.0676***	−0.0569**	−0.0771**
	(0.0006)	(0.0029)	(0.0016)	(0.0040)	(0.0098)	(0.0125)	(0.0118)	(0.0193)	(0.0266)	(0.0380)
Hispanic female	−0.0029	−0.0179***	0.0017	−0.0185**	−0.0473**	−0.0180	0.0255	−0.0637	−0.0958	0.1313
	(0.0020)	(0.0055)	(0.0020)	(0.0083)	(0.0222)	(0.0268)	(0.0221)	(0.0433)	(0.0690)	(0.0955)
Other minority female	−0.0019**	−0.0091***	−0.0021	−0.0165***	−0.0370***	−0.0366**	−0.0043	−0.0331	−0.0875	0.1662**
	(0.0010)	(0.0032)	(0.0020)	(0.0059)	(0.0142)	(0.0180)	(0.0190)	(0.0314)	(0.0562)	(0.0728)
Occupation: Intelligence	−0.0001	0.0044***	0.0010	−0.0188***	−0.0442***	0.0426***	0.0129***	−0.0153*	−0.0260**	0.0263*
	(0.0003)	(0.0008)	(0.0007)	(0.0029)	(0.0053)	(0.0052)	(0.0046)	(0.0079)	(0.0104)	(0.0148)
Occupation: Engineering and maintenance	0.0000	0.0033***	−0.0001	−0.0204***	−0.0846***	0.0155***	0.0026	−0.0126**	−0.0232***	0.0446***
	(0.0002)	(0.0006)	(0.0005)	(0.0019)	(0.0040)	(0.0040)	(0.0037)	(0.0059)	(0.0071)	(0.0101)
Occupation: Administration	0.0001	−0.0017	−0.0018**	−0.0162***	−0.0560***	0.0375***	0.0172***	−0.0010	−0.0243***	0.0392***
	(0.0002)	(0.0011)	(0.0008)	(0.0025)	(0.0053)	(0.0051)	(0.0045)	(0.0075)	(0.0090)	(0.0130)
Occupation: Supply and procurement	−0.0004	−0.0019*	−0.0008	−0.0273***	−0.0636***	0.0344***	0.0349***	0.0192***	−0.0400***	0.0135
	(0.0003)	(0.0010)	(0.0006)	(0.0022)	(0.0045)	(0.0044)	(0.0036)	(0.0062)	(0.0079)	(0.0112)
Occupation: Other	−0.0000	−0.0044***	−0.0019***	0.0190***	−0.0353***	0.0350***	0.0367***	−0.0591**	−0.0446	−0.0375
	(0.0002)	(0.0010)	(0.0007)	(0.0016)	(0.0080)	(0.0078)	(0.0116)	(0.0254)	(0.0439)	(0.0560)

Table A.5—Continued

Variable	(1) Retention as O1	(2) Promotion to O2	(3) Retention as O2	(4) Promotion to O3	(5) Retention as O3	(6) Promotion to O4	(7) Retention as O4	(8) Promotion to O5	(9) Retention as O5	(10) Promotion to O6
Cumulative months of deployment	0.0005*	0.0013***	0.0003***	0.0014***	−0.0005*	0.0020***	0.0006***	−0.0009***	0.0003	0.0046***
	(0.0003)	(0.0001)	(0.0001)	(0.0001)	(0.0002)	(0.0001)	(0.0001)	(0.0002)	(0.0003)	(0.0003)
Married	−0.0005**	0.0010	0.0012***	0.0124***	0.0527***	0.0303***	0.0032	0.0571***	−0.0141*	0.0388***
	(0.0002)	(0.0006)	(0.0004)	(0.0011)	(0.0026)	(0.0029)	(0.0036)	(0.0059)	(0.0079)	(0.0123)
Less than baccalaureate	0.0001	−0.0001	−0.0005	0.0209***	0.1369***	−0.0056	−0.0473***	−0.0417***	−0.0919***	−0.1280***
	(0.0002)	(0.0008)	(0.0009)	(0.0022)	(0.0060)	(0.0074)	(0.0097)	(0.0155)	(0.0280)	(0.0409)
More than baccalaureate	−0.0001	−0.0066***	−0.0044***	0.0094***	0.0066	0.0506***	0.0257***	0.0792***	−0.0029	0.0970***
	(0.0004)	(0.0020)	(0.0015)	(0.0031)	(0.0055)	(0.0053)	(0.0028)	(0.0042)	(0.0060)	(0.0085)
Observations	143,850	154,189	152,447	178,338	141,493	95,560	56,510	49,656	30,232	23,996

NOTE: Standard errors in parentheses. Table shows marginal effects evaluated at the mean values of the other covariates. All models include year-of-entry fixed effects. *** = statistically significant from zero at the 1 percent level; ** = statistically significant from zero at the 5 percent level; * = statistically significant from zero at the 10 percent level.

Table A.6
Probit Regression Estimates of Minority and Gender Differences in Achieving O4, and in Achieving O6, Conditional on Having Reached O4

Variable	(1) O1 to O4 Promotion	(2) O4 to O6 Promotion
Prior service	0.1161***	−0.1170***
	(0.0046)	(0.0082)
Navy	−0.0288***	−0.0126
	(0.0059)	(0.0103)
Marine Corps	−0.0361***	−0.0290
	(0.0079)	(0.0211)
Air Force	0.1444***	−0.1143***
	(0.0046)	(0.0092)
ROTC	0.0260***	−0.0390***
	(0.0038)	(0.0090)
Officer Candidate School/Training	0.0155***	−0.0821***
	(0.0057)	(0.0095)
Direct appointment	0.0279***	−0.0753***
	(0.0107)	(0.0149)
Unknown or other source of commission	0.0788***	−0.0659***
	(0.0099)	(0.0232)
Black male	0.0176***	−0.0402***
	(0.0063)	(0.0144)
Hispanic male	0.0043	−0.0343
	(0.0087)	(0.0240)
Other minority male	0.0296***	−0.0257
	(0.0067)	(0.0189)
White female	−0.1463***	−0.0472***
	(0.0052)	(0.0136)
Black female	−0.0011	−0.0786***
	(0.0122)	(0.0262)
Hispanic female	−0.0894***	−0.0054
	(0.0232)	(0.0772)
Other minority female	−0.0815***	0.0316
	(0.0150)	(0.0614)

Table A.6—Continued

	(1)	(2)
Variable	O1 to O4 Promotion	O4 to O6 Promotion
General/flag officer, executive	−0.0337	
	(0.0666)	
Occupation: Intelligence	−0.0287***	−0.0126
	(0.0075)	(0.0136)
Occupation: Engineering and maintenance	−0.0639***	−0.0043
	(0.0052)	(0.0104)
Occupation: Administration	−0.0120*	0.0196
	(0.0071)	(0.0151)
Occupation: Supply and procurement	−0.0465***	0.0039
	(0.0063)	(0.0118)
Occupation: Other	−0.0072	0.0994
	(0.0058)	(0.0608)
Cumulative months of deployment	0.0082	0.0014***
	(0.0053)	(0.0004)
Married	0.0908***	0.0288***
	(0.0046)	(0.0098)
Less than baccalaureate	0.1115***	−0.0586*
	(0.0064)	(0.0328)
More than baccalaureate	0.0562***	0.0585***
	(0.0118)	(0.0076)
Observations	117,032	15,759

NOTE: Standard errors in parentheses. Table shows marginal effects evaluated at the mean values of the other covariates. All models include year-of-entry fixed effects. *** = statistically significant from zero at the 1 percent level; ** = statistically significant from zero at the 5 percent level; * = statistically significant from zero at the 10 percent level.

Table A.7
Probit Regression Estimates of Career Progression of Women in Partially Closed Occupations

Variable	(1) Retention as O3	(2) Promotion to O4	(3) Retention as O4	(4) Promotion to O5	(5) Retention as O5	(6) Promotion to O6
Female	-0.1053***	-0.0288***	-0.0280***	0.0059	-0.1078***	0.0142
	(0.0049)	(0.0061)	(0.0059)	(0.0079)	(0.0113)	(0.0148)
Partially closed occupation	-0.0841***	0.0458***	0.0185***	0.0081	-0.0527***	0.0306*
	(0.0041)	(0.0047)	(0.0041)	(0.0075)	(0.0136)	(0.0182)
Female in partially closed occupation	0.0617***	-0.0316**	-0.0163	0.0052	-0.0131	-0.0470
	(0.0093)	(0.0156)	(0.0161)	(0.0246)	(0.0349)	(0.0614)
Prior service	0.0857***	0.0166***	-0.0904***	-0.1424***	-0.1506***	-0.0093
	(0.0035)	(0.0041)	(0.0042)	(0.0057)	(0.0075)	(0.0100)
Navy	-0.0248***	-0.1178***	-0.0470***	-0.0986***	0.0622***	-0.0210*
	(0.0036)	(0.0048)	(0.0044)	(0.0068)	(0.0073)	(0.0113)
Marine Corps	0.0632***	-0.0935***	-0.0300***	-0.1383***	-0.0062	0.0357
	(0.0056)	(0.0078)	(0.0078)	(0.0134)	(0.0255)	(0.0367)
Air Force	0.0650***	-0.0225***	-0.0200***	-0.1499***	-0.0228***	-0.1142***
	(0.0034)	(0.0043)	(0.0042)	(0.0067)	(0.0074)	(0.0108)
ROTC	0.0592***	0.0019	0.0079**	-0.0697***	-0.0225***	-0.0758***
	(0.0031)	(0.0039)	(0.0035)	(0.0056)	(0.0065)	(0.0084)
Officer Candidate School/Training	0.0720***	-0.0222***	-0.0183***	-0.1202***	-0.0895***	-0.0939***
	(0.0039)	(0.0050)	(0.0044)	(0.0071)	(0.0080)	(0.0097)

Table A.7—Continued

Variable	(1) Retention as O3	(2) Promotion to O4	(3) Retention as O4	(4) Promotion to O5	(5) Retention as O5	(6) Promotion to O6
Direct appointment	0.0682***	−0.0010	−0.0395***	−0.1071***	−0.0917***	−0.0893***
	(0.0070)	(0.0085)	(0.0073)	(0.0113)	(0.0127)	(0.0141)
Unknown or other source of commission	0.1017***	−0.0013	−0.0477***	−0.0649***	0.0547**	−0.1588***
	(0.0070)	(0.0090)	(0.0129)	(0.0197)	(0.0245)	(0.0362)
Occupation: Intelligence	−0.0192***	0.0307***	0.0111**	−0.0044	−0.0192*	0.0135
	(0.0053)	(0.0061)	(0.0048)	(0.0081)	(0.0104)	(0.0146)
Occupation: Engineering and maintenance	−0.0771***	0.0104**	0.0045	−0.0012	−0.0212***	0.0197**
	(0.0040)	(0.0044)	(0.0037)	(0.0059)	(0.0071)	(0.0098)
Occupation: Administration	−0.0437***	0.0283***	0.0192***	0.0105	−0.0186**	0.0121
	(0.0053)	(0.0057)	(0.0045)	(0.0076)	(0.0089)	(0.0127)
Occupation: Supply and procurement	−0.0522***	0.0272***	0.0366***	0.0233***	−0.0352***	−0.0005
	(0.0045)	(0.0050)	(0.0036)	(0.0064)	(0.0079)	(0.0110)
Occupation: Other	−0.0376***	0.0379***	0.0367***	−0.0559**	−0.0396	−0.0562
	(0.0080)	(0.0085)	(0.0117)	(0.0252)	(0.0434)	(0.0536)
Cumulative months of deployment	−0.0002	0.0024***	0.0006***	0.0010***	0.0003	−0.0001
	(0.0002)	(0.0003)	(0.0001)	(0.0002)	(0.0003)	(0.0004)
Married	0.0496***	0.0342***	0.0019	0.0717***	−0.0148*	0.0451***
	(0.0026)	(0.0031)	(0.0036)	(0.0060)	(0.0079)	(0.0119)
Less than baccalaureate	0.1344***	0.0028	−0.0479***	−0.0191	−0.0888***	−0.1229***
	(0.0061)	(0.0079)	(0.0098)	(0.0156)	(0.0280)	(0.0397)

Table A.7—Continued

Variable	(1) Retention as O3	(2) Promotion to O4	(3) Retention as O4	(4) Promotion to O5	(5) Retention as O5	(6) Promotion to O6
More than baccalaureate	0.0063	0.0571***	0.0268***	0.0972***	–0.0037	0.0944***
	(0.0055)	(0.0058)	(0.0028)	(0.0043)	(0.0060)	(0.0083)
Observations	138,357	96,278	55,500	50,252	30,060	24,795

NOTE: Standard errors in parentheses. Table shows marginal effects evaluated at the mean values of the other covariates. All models include year-of-entry fixed effects. *** = statistically significant from zero at the 1 percent level; ** = statistically significant from zero at the 5 percent level; * = statistically significant from zero at the 10 percent level.

Table A.8
Probit Regression Estimates of Likelihood of Reaching O4, and of Reaching O6, Conditional on Having Reached O4, for Women in Partially Closed Occupations

Variable	(1) O1 to O4 Promotion	(2) O4 to O6 Promotion
Female	−0.1311***	−0.0406***
	(0.0051)	(0.0135)
Partially closed occupation	0.0864***	−0.0131
	(0.0136)	(0.0365)
Female in partially closed occupation	0.0703***	0.0169
	(0.0047)	(0.0119)
Prior service	0.1177***	−0.1182***
	(0.0047)	(0.0082)
Navy	−0.0231***	−0.0083
	(0.0059)	(0.0104)
Marine Corps	−0.0617***	−0.0294
	(0.0082)	(0.0252)
Air Force	0.1651***	−0.1081***
	(0.0047)	(0.0097)
ROTC	0.0261***	−0.0374***
	(0.0038)	(0.0090)
Officer Candidate School/Training	0.0140**	−0.0804***
	(0.0058)	(0.0096)
Direct appointment	0.0376***	−0.0696***
	(0.0108)	(0.0153)
Unknown or other source of commission	0.0917***	−0.0676**
	(0.0103)	(0.0274)
Occupation: Intelligence	−0.0509***	−0.0151
	(0.0075)	(0.0138)
Occupation: Engineering and maintenance	−0.0700***	−0.0074
	(0.0053)	(0.0103)
Occupation: Administration	−0.0208***	0.0147
	(0.0071)	(0.0151)
Occupation: Supply and procurement	−0.0477***	0.0001
	(0.0063)	(0.0117)

Table A.8—Continued

	(1)	(2)
Variable	O1 to O4 Promotion	O4 to O6 Promotion
Occupation: Other	−0.0101*	0.0962
	(0.0058)	(0.0605)
Cumulative months of deployment	0.0071	0.0014***
	(0.0053)	(0.0004)
Married	0.0890***	0.0314***
	(0.0046)	(0.0099)
Less than baccalaureate	0.1157***	−0.0574*
	(0.0066)	(0.0330)
More than baccalaureate	0.0573***	0.0613***
	(0.0119)	(0.0076)
Observations	114,675	15,488

NOTE: Standard errors in parentheses. Table shows marginal effects evaluated at the mean values of the other covariates. All models include year-of-entry fixed effects. *** = statistically significant from zero at the 1 percent level; ** = statistically significant from zero at the 5 percent level; * = statistically significant from zero at the 10 percent level.

References

Asch, Beth J., James Hosek, and John T. Warner, *An Analysis of Pay for Enlisted Personnel*, Santa Monica, Calif.: RAND Corporation, DB-344-OSD, 2001. As of August 15, 2011:
http://www.rand.org/pubs/documented_briefings/DB344.html

Asch, Beth, and John Warner, "A Theory of Compensation and Personnel Policy in Hierarchical Organizations with Application to the United States Military," *Journal of Labor Economics*, Vol. 19, No. 3, July 2001, pp. 523–562.

Buddin, Richard, Daniel S. Levy, Janet M. Hanley, and Donald Waldman, *Promotion Tempo and Enlisted Retention*, Santa Monica, Calif.: RAND Corporation, R-4135-FMP, 1992. As of September 4, 2011:
http://www.rand.org/pubs/reports/R4135.html

Congressional Budget Office, *The Drawdown of the Military Officer Corps*, Washington, D.C., CBO Paper, November 1999. As of August 23, 2011:
http://www.cbo.gov/ftpdocs/17xx/doc1772/drawdown.pdf

Department of Defense, *Career Progression of Minority and Women Officers*, Office of the Under Secretary of Defense, Personnel and Readiness, 1999. As of August 15, 2011:
http://mldc.whs.mil/download/documents/CNA%20Publications%20and%20Graphics/Publications/Pipeline%20Study%201999.pdf

———, *Population Representation in the Military Services, Fiscal Year 2009*, Washington, D.C.: U.S. Government Printing Office, 2011. As of August 15, 2011:
http://prhome.defense.gov/RFM/MPP/ACCESSION%20POLICY/poprep.aspx

Fricker, Ronald D., *The Effect of Perstempo on Officer Retention in the U.S. Military*, Santa Monica, Calif.: RAND Corporation, MR-1556-OSD, 2002. As of September 2, 2011:
http://www.rand.org/pubs/monograph_reports/MR1556.html

Hansen, Michael L., and Jennie W. Wenger, *Why Do Pay Elasticities Differ?* Alexandria, Va.: CNA, CRM D0005644.A2/Final, 2002.

Harrell, Margaret C., Laura Werber Casteneda, Peter Schirmer, Bryan W. Hallmark, Jennifer Kavanagh, Daniel Gershwin, and Paul Steinberg, *Assessing the Assignment Policy for Army Women*, Santa Monica, Calif.: RAND Corporation, MG-590-1-OSD, 2007. As of August 25, 2011:
http://www.rand.org/pubs/monographs/MG590-1.html

Harrell, Margaret C., Megan K. Beckett, Chiaying Sandy Chien, and Jerry M. Sollinger, *The Status of Gender Integration in the Military: Analysis of Selected Occupations*, Santa Monica, Calif.: RAND Corporation, MR-1380-OSD, 2002. As of August 25, 2011:
http://www.rand.org/pubs/monograph_reports/MR1380.html

Harrell, Margaret C., and Laura L. Miller, *New Opportunities for Military Women: Effects upon Readiness, Cohesion, and Morale*, Santa Monica, Calif.: RAND Corporation, MR-896-OSD, 1997. As of August 25, 2011:
http://www.rand.org/pubs/monograph_reports/MR896.html

Hosek, James, and Paco Martorell, *How Have Deployments During the War on Terrorism Affected Reenlistment?* Santa Monica, Calif.: RAND Corporation, MG-873-OSD, 2009. As of August 15, 2011:
http://www.rand.org/pubs/monographs/MG873.html

Hosek, James, and Mark E. Totten, *Does Perstempo Hurt Reenlistment? The Effect of Long or Hostile Perstempo on Reenlistment*, Santa Monica, Calif.: RAND Corporation, MR-990-OSD, 1998. As of September 28, 2011:
http://www.rand.org/pubs/monograph_reports/MR990.html

Hosek, Susan D., Peter Tiemeyer, M. Rebecca Kilburn, Debra A. Strong, Selika Ducksworth, and Reginald Ray, *Minority and Gender Differences in Officer Career Progression*, Santa Monica, Calif.: RAND Corporation, MR-1184-OSD, 2001. As of August 15, 2011:
http://www.rand.org/pubs/monograph_reports/MR1184.html

Hubbard, William, "Supplemental Appendix: The Phantom Gender Difference in the College Wage Premium," University of Chicago Working Paper, November 2009. As of August 23, 2011:
http://home.uchicago.edu/~whhubbar/PhantomAppx.pdf

Lim, Nelson, Michelle Cho, and Kimberly Curry Hall, *Planning for Diversity: Options and Recommendations for DoD Leaders*, Santa Monica, Calif.: RAND Corporation, MG-743-OSD, 2008. As of August 15, 2011:
http://www.rand.org/pubs/monographs/MG743.html

Mattock, Michael G., James Hosek, and Beth J. Asch, *Reserve Participation and Cost Under a New Approach to Reserve Compensation*, Santa Monica, Calif.: RAND Corporation, forthcoming.

Military Leadership Diversity Commission, *From Representation to Inclusion: Diversity Leadership for the 21st Century Military, Final Report*, Arlington, Va., 2011. As of August 15, 2011:
http://mldc.whs.mil/index.php/final-report

Miller, Laura L., Jennifer Kavanagh, Maria C. Lytell, Keith Jennings, and Craig Martin, *The Extent of Restrictions on the Service of Active Component Military Women*, Santa Monica, Calif.: RAND Corporation, forthcoming.

Passel, Jeffrey S., D'Vera Cohn, and Mark Hugo Lopez, *Census 2010: 50 Million Latinos, Hispanics Account for More Than Half of Nation's Growth in Past Decade*, Washington, D.C.: Pew Research Center, March 24, 2011. As of August 23, 2011:
http://www.pewhispanic.org/reports/report.php?ReportID=140

Public Law 111-383, National Defense Authorization Act for Fiscal Year 2011, January 7, 2011.

White House, Office of Management and Budget, *Guidance on Aggregation and Allocation of Data on Race for Use in Civil Rights Monitoring and Enforcement*, OMB Bulletin No. 00-02, March 9, 2000. As of August 15, 2011:
http://www.whitehouse.gov/omb/bulletins_b00-02